CREATIVE EMBROIDERY
a complete guide

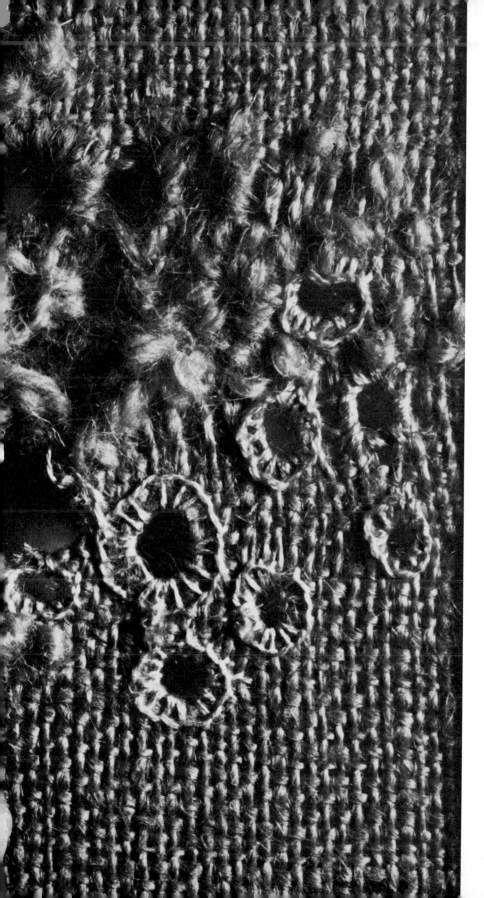

CREATIVE EMBROIDERY
a complete guide

Anne Spence

Nelson

This book was designed and produced by
George Rainbird Ltd
Marble Arch House, 44 Edgware Road, London W2

First published in Great Britain in 1975 by
Thomas Nelson and Sons Ltd
36 Park Street, London W1Y 4DE

Nelson (Africa) Ltd
P.O. Box 18123, Nairobi, Kenya

Thomas Nelson (Australia) Ltd
19-39 Jeffcott Street, West Melbourne 3003

Thomas Nelson and Sons (Canada) Ltd
81 Curlew Drive, Don Mills, Ontario

Thomas Nelson (Nigeria) Ltd
P.O. Box 336, Apapa, Lagos

House Editor: Erica Hunningher
Associate House Editor: Felicity Luard
Designer: Pauline Harrison
Index by: Myra Clark

Colour plates originated by Alabaster Passmore
Text printed and bound by A. Wheaton & Company, Exeter

ISBN: 0 17 149048 7

Frontispiece and title page: Experiment in texture,
Goldsmiths' College, School of Art, London

Contents

Acknowledgments

The author wishes to thank all those who have kindly allowed their work to be reproduced. Constance Howard for reading the manuscript and for her permission to photograph and reproduce the work of students at Goldsmiths' College, School of Art, London. Erica Hunningher for her generous cooperation and support. Ione Dorrington for her assistance in several matters and John Hunnex for the superb photography of the colour plates as well as the black-and-white photographs.

Introduction

Our age of materialism, technology and mass-production has created a climate in which many individuals feel that their identity has somehow been suppressed. Because of this they are motivated to express their individualism in a personal way and for many people the art of creating a visual statement is a way of achieving this sense of identity.

Embroidery is a means of personal expression, as well as a stimulating and rewarding art form. Using fabric and thread the embroiderer can express the sheer delight of decorative invention, involving the aesthetic qualities of relationships between colour, shape and texture and an emotional response to visual and intellectual stimuli.

The greater part of this book is concerned with the craft or techniques of embroidery. (The term embroidery is used to denote a wide variety of methods of working with fabric and thread and is not restricted simply to stitchery.) This aspect of the subject is emphasized in an attempt to introduce the uninitiated to the tremendous variety of effects which can be created with fabric and thread. It is hoped that the reader will use these techniques as a vocabulary or foundation for evolving original and imaginative designs.

1 Design

THEMES FOR DESIGN AND SOURCES OF IDEAS

Any subject which stimulates the creative individual to translate experience into visual form is valid. Themes for embroidery, as for other art forms, may be drawn from the physical or intellectual environment or the inner world of the imagination.

Study and observation of the physical environment will suggest a profusion of different themes. Varieties of shape, pattern, texture and colour combinations can be seen in both natural and man-made objects. Plants, trees, rock strata, minerals, animals, birds and insects are a rich source of material. The superb structure, texture and colour observed in such natural features as mountain ranges, canyons and rift valleys may stimulate the creation of numerous effects. Shape and pattern also exist in abundance in buildings, in machines and equipment, in fact in any mechanical device or object created by man. Through sensitivity and awareness the embroiderer will discover inspiration in the most mundane objects.

Both shape and colour can be associated with emotional and physical sensations. Jagged lines and sharp angular shapes evoke feelings of force, energy and violence, while simple rectilinear shapes suggest a more subdued or calm feeling. Shape often stimulates a sensation of movement: curvilinear shapes appear to move or flow whereas rectilinear shapes appear relatively static. Compare, for example, flowing water or flickering flames, and the static shapes of buildings. This observation may be extended to include rhythm, which is closely connected with movement. Shapes placed with different intervals or spaces between them create a kind of rhythm as the eye travels from one shape to the next.

Colour is often described as hot or cold, dreary or jazzy and these associations with physical and emotional sensations can be used and developed when creating designs. These would not necessarily resemble any part of the physical world, they might, rather, be abstract – with shape and colour suggesting violence, heat, calm and peace.

Themes drawn from the inner world of the imagination are the product of unconscious impulses and intuitive judgment. Personal imagery probably grows out of the subjective development in the mind of the more tangible experience of the visual and physical world.

8

Spontaneous designs based on personal imagery can be cultivated.

There are many ways of developing a theme based on visual stimuli. The shape of an object, for example, might be the starting point for a design. It could be enlarged, reduced, repeated, assembled and arranged into new patterns and structures. A small section of the object might be isolated, and details of pattern, shape, colour and texture of that area emphasized. Conversely, a large-scale subject, perhaps a landscape or city, might be simplified to broad outlines and major shapes. Texture is another starting point, and an interesting design might be developed on the theme of contrasting textures.

Information for designs can be obtained in various ways. Drawing is one method of gathering information, and a means whereby shape, structure, pattern and texture can be described. Drawing is a valuable experience: it cultivates the ability to see, and develops a greater understanding and awareness of shape and form, space and structure. A deeper appreciation of the physical world provides more varied stimulation and greater scope for producing original and personal designs.

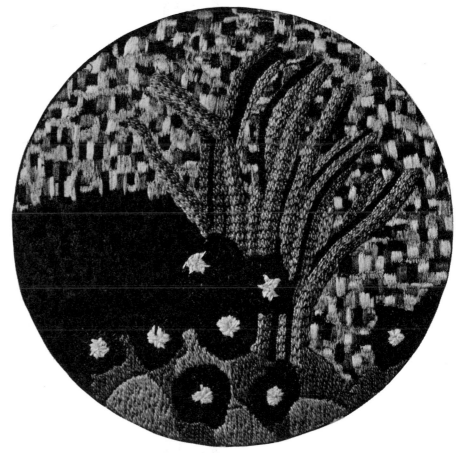

A profusion of different themes can be found in the varieties of shape, pattern, texture and colour combinations of objects in the physical environment – however mundane or ordinary. Drawing is a valuable way of collecting and recording this information, which can later be translated into fabric and thread. Pencil and crayon sketch and machine and hand embroidery by Kirsten Hamilton-Fairley, 8 in. (25 mm) diameter.

If you find drawing difficult, you may be able to overcome certain problems by rationalizing your approach. For example, in initial experiments describe different aspects of an object separately. In the first drawing describe the overall shape, outline or structure. These can be simply drawn, and the points where different planes converge merely indicated. In a second drawing show the secondary shapes and patterns. In further drawings continue to introduce additional details of shape and pattern within the main structure. Begin with simple forms and objects, and gradually proceed to more complex shapes.

Produce a variety of effects by experimenting with different media, pencil, ink, charcoal, chalk, wax and oil crayons, used singly or in combination. Wax and oil crayons, coloured pencils and designers' gouache are particularly successful for colour studies. Use a sketchbook regularly and this will provide a constant supply of starting points for design. Carry it with you and record any object, shape or pattern that seems interesting.

Information can also be collected by other means. The camera is a marvellous tool for building a visual record, and provides an easier method of capturing moving subject matter. Magazines and newspaper cuttings are a valuable source of information and can be collected for their colour, shape and pattern content. Scientific, zoological and botanical magazines are rich in visual information, often showing microscopic detail which might be an interesting starting point for a design.

THE BASIC PRINCIPLES OF DESIGN

The artist or designer does not reproduce visual experiences exactly, but rather interprets and translates them according to subjective and intuitive judgment. The end product is an amalgamation of what is seen and felt, but an understanding of the basic principles of pictorial expression will help in the development of these responses. Basic principles, however, are not formulae for creating successful designs nor are they rules which must be obeyed. They are simply a means of understanding and controlling the visual elements of design. Many people have a natural ability to make coherent visual statements without conscious recourse to these principles; others may find the process of designing more stimulating or rewarding if basic principles are brought into conscious use.

Shape
Shape will be considered in the context of the two-dimensional picture area or ground. It can be described in outline or expressed in colour,

(*above*) The significance of a small shape is decreased by being on a large ground as it appears to contract. A large shape appears to expand and dominates the picture area.

(*right*) Sensations of movement are created by placing a shape in different positions within a picture area.

texture and line. A continuous line, whether drawn or made with thread, indicates an area and the meeting of two points of such a line suggests a shape. A similar shape could be described with separate lines, placed within an imaginary outline. If the lines were placed at definite intervals and angles to each other the shape could be said to be described by a pattern. Texture and colour used in relation to shape and design can produce a sense of space (see pages 17 and 15).

Shape does not exist in isolation. Immediately a shape is formed on a ground, a relationship operates between the shape and the edge of the picture area. A visual energy and space is created. The area of ground between the shape and the edge of the picture area is as important as the shape itself. It provides a framework in which the shape exists and influences it to a lesser or greater degree. A small shape placed in a large picture area will appear to contract, as the surrounding area overwhelms and reduces its significance. A larger shape that almost fills the total picture space will appear to expand and dominate the picture area.

The position of a shape within the picture area brings other factors into play. A shape placed near the top of the picture area, for example, creates a sense of upward movement. A shape placed near the lower edge pulls the eye downwards. Horizontal movement is suggested when the shape is positioned to one side. A more complex situation is created when two shapes are placed within the picture area. The eye is forced to scan backwards and forwards between the two while at the same time recognizing their combined positions within the picture. When many shapes are formed within the picture, the sense of movement is strengthened.

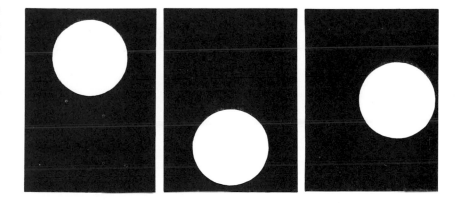

It is essential when planning an embroidery to consider carefully the position and arrangement of shapes, as this is of vital importance to the whole design. Formal logical arrangements usually suggest order and control, while loose and erratic arrangements are more ambiguous,

11

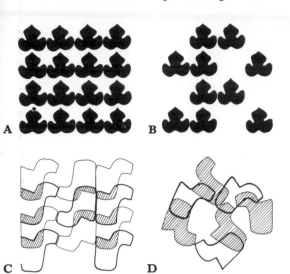

A   B

C   D

(*above*) **A** Repeat pattern with the shapes placed in even rows. **B** The distance or space between the shapes is altered. **C** A shape overlapped many times to create a regular pattern. **D** The same shape overlapped to create a random effect.

(*right*) Complex effects of movement are created in a simple repeat pattern by contrasting lines of straight stitches (page 94) worked in different directions, which force the eye to scan backwards and forwards and up and down over the picture area. The vertical lines of applied ribbon unite the elements of the design by drawing the eye back towards the centre. *Graphic Spot* by Mary Newlands, 14 × 15 in. (355 × 380 mm).

(*far right*) **A** A design of interlocking shapes. **B** Shapes grouped together in a regular pattern. **C** Shapes grouped together and placed at random within the picture area. **D** Shapes of different sizes.

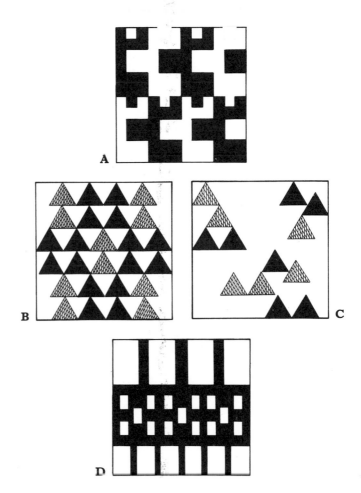

suggesting less order and more freedom. Shapes can be repeated, inter-locked and overlapped. A simple repeat pattern is created when one shape or unit is repeated in even rows vertically and horizontally to the picture area. Variation can be created by altering the distance between the shapes. More complex arrangements might be constructed with groups of shapes, repeated at regular intervals or distributed at random within the picture area. Interesting effects can be achieved with different-sized shapes; smaller shapes might alternate with larger ones to achieve greater contrast. The jigsaw puzzle is an excellent example of inter-locking shapes, and the same principle can be applied to an embroidery design.

When planning a design based on overlapping shapes, it may be useful to experiment first with tissue paper. Cut out several shapes and observe the new shapes which appear where overlapping occurs. This effect can be used to advantage in embroidery as transparent fabrics will give similar results. Overlapped shapes drawn in outline also produce secondary shapes; similarly, when shapes are cut from opaque material and overlapped, the form of the underlying shapes is lost and new shapes are created.

The distribution of shapes should be considered carefully, for they create important subdivisions in the picture space. The size and proportions of these subdivisions (shapes) are vital factors influencing the initial impact of a design. If it is divided in unequal proportions by a variety of shapes of different sizes, it will probably give an impression of intricacy or complexity. Conversely, a design divided by similar shapes of equal size will give an initial impression of simplicity.

Dividing the picture area by means of straight and curved lines is one way of achieving abstract designs based on area division. Lines can be placed vertically, horizontally and diagonally to the picture area in a variety of ways, dividing it into stripes, squares, rectangles, triangles, etc. An element of contrast is introduced when shapes of different size are combined within one design.

Shapes within a picture area may appear to advance or recede. The size, colour, tone and distribution of shapes have a combined influence on their spatial significance. Small embroidery by Pamela Whatmore, satin stitch in coton perlé (pearl cotton) and crewel wool on a striped cotton fabric, $4\frac{3}{4} \times 6\frac{1}{4}$ in. (120 × 160 mm).

Shapes within a picture area may appear to advance or recede. The colour, tone and distribution of shapes have a combined influence on their spatial significance. For example, if several small black shapes were placed around one large black shape on a white background, the large shape would appear to advance from the smaller shapes. If the large shape were pale in colour, the smaller shapes would advance. When many different sized shapes are combined in a design more complex spatial relationships occur.

Colour

The use of colour in design is generally considered to be based on subjective judgment. And while colour schemes based on personal preferences do contribute much to the originality and individuality of a design, there are theories of colour which may be studied in order to appreciate the factors operating in pictorial expression.

We are concerned here with colour transmitted through a pigment: either paint or dye. The study of colour transmitted through rays of light is left to the physicist. The objective study of colour is begun by establishing the essential characteristics of colour: hue, tone and saturation. Hue is the quality that distinguishes one colour from another, for example blue from violet. Tone is the quality of brightness, for example light or dark tones of blue. Saturation is the quality of strength or purity of colour.

A sound introduction to the theory of colour is to experiment with mixing the three primary colours – red, yellow and blue. From these primary colours, secondary and tertiary colours are obtained. A secondary colour is the result of mixing the primary colours as follows:

red + yellow = orange
yellow + blue = green
red + blue = violet

The three secondary colours must be mixed carefully. Each secondary colour is established half way between two primary colours – orange must be neither too red nor too yellow.

Tertiary colours result from mixing a primary colour with a secondary colour:

yellow + orange = yellow-orange
red + orange = red-orange
red + violet = red-violet
blue + violet = blue-violet
blue + green = blue-green
yellow + green = yellow-green

It will be appreciated that many other tertiary colours can be made by intermixing these colours. White added to these colours will produce tints, and the addition of black will produce shades. An unlimited range of colours can be mixed from a palette of red, yellow, blue, black and white.

Apart from mixing pigment to obtain colours there is another method, known as visual mixing. This involves placing small dots of pure colour adjacent to each other over an area. When viewed from a distance the dots appear to blend and form one colour and tones achieved by this form of mixing appear more vibrant. In painting this method is known as the pointillist technique. This phenomenon is of great interest and value to the embroiderer; the dots of paint can be replaced by stitches such as the french knot and bullion knot.

Colour appears to change in different contexts, when placed near or surrounded by another colour, for example. If a red square is placed on a white background and another identical red square is placed on a black background, the red will appear darker and weaker on the white and more luminous and warm on the black. Similarly, a yellow square on white will appear darker than the same yellow square on black.

It is particularly important to consider the interrelationship of colours when translating a black and white design, drawing or photograph into colour, as the significance of shape is reduced or strengthened by colour. When a large yellow shape and several small violet shapes are placed on a white background, for example, the larger shape appears to recede into the background and the smaller shapes to advance and dominate the area. The reverse effect occurs when the large shape is violet in colour and the smaller shapes yellow. When both dull pale tones and dark tones are placed on a white background, pale tones appear to recede and dark tones advance from the background. But on a black background the effects are again different: dark tones appear to recede and pale tones advance.

The characteristics of colour effects are based on seven different kinds of contrast:

1 Contrast of hue is easily appreciated, as it is the difference in colour. Red, yellow and blue are the extreme examples of such contrast. Less contrast exists between secondary colours and it is further diminished between tertiary colours.

2 Contrast of light and dark is more readily recognized between tones of one colour, between light green and dark green, for example. The admixture of white or black to lighten or darken a colour reduces the vividness of the hue. Pure colour differs in brilliance. Pure yellow is a light colour, it cannot be darkened and remain pure. Pure blue is essentially a dark colour; light blue is dim and pale. Red is forceful when dark but loses its vitality when lightened.

3 Warm-cold contrast: generally, yellow, yellow-orange, orange, red-orange, red and red-violet are referred to as warm or hot. Yellow-green,

green, green-blue, blue, blue-violet, and violet are referred to as cold colours. Blue-green and red-orange represent the extreme opposites in cold-warm contrast. The 'temperature' of a colour is strengthened or weakened according to the colour surrounding or adjacent to it. Red appears hotter when surrounded by a cold colour, but less so when surrounded by a warm colour. Cold-warm contrast is often associated with a sense of space, in general terms cold colours appear to recede and warm colours to advance.

4 Complementary contrast: two colours are complementary if by mixture they yield a neutral grey-black: blue-orange, red-green, yellow-violet, for example. Complementary colours oppose and excite each other. Adjacent complementaries enhance each other to maximum vividness; they neutralize each other when mixed.

5 Simultaneous contrast occurs as a sensation in the mind and eye. It can be illustrated by placing one medium-grey square on red and another, of similar size, on green. In each case the grey square will appear tinged with the complementary of the colour on which it is placed: grey on green will appear tinged with red and the grey on red tinged with green.

6 Contrast of saturation is the contrast between pure colour and mixed colour. To appreciate the nature of this contrast more easily mix a colour with white, black and grey. When pure colour and mixed colour are juxtaposed, the mixed colours appear to gain vitality and the pure colours to lose some of their force.

7 Contrast of extension is essentially a matter of proportion, that is, the relationship between coloured areas of different size. When a small area of colour is surrounded by a larger area of a different colour, the effect of the smaller area is more intense than it would be if surrounded by an equal amount of the other colour.

For the first experiments in the objective study of colour, exercises should be carried out in a simple checkerboard, rectangular or striped pattern, to avoid the danger of becoming involved in experiments with shape. The analysis of colour in natural form will reveal many marvellous colour schemes. There need be no attempt to suggest the shape and form of the object, but rather to extract the quality and relationship of colours. To be of value such colour studies should aim to achieve a proportion and intensity of colour similar to that in the original source.

Texture

The term texture is often used to describe an uneven surface. Bark may be described as textured, whereas glass is said to have a smooth surface. The texture of a surface is formed by the structure of the material from which it is made. The texture of a leaf is the direct result of its particular

vein structure. The texture of plain weave, pile, knitted or bonded fabric is as much the result of the structure as of the threads from which it is formed.

In principle we could conceive texture as separate parts united into a whole. If we accept this statement, we must apply it to the construction of texture in embroidery. An area of texture, developed out of fabric, thread and beads, for example, should give a unified overall effect. If any one of the parts appears to stand out from the others, it will be seen as a separate entity. A few beads widely dispersed over a large area are seen as individual shapes whereas many beads massed together will be seen as a texture, each bead becoming part of the total effect.

Contrast of texture, like contrast of colours, is perceived by means of comparison. A rough texture is more effective when adjacent to or surrounded by a finer texture. The character of texture is not destroyed by a change of colour in the constituent material. The texture of a piece of bark would be the same whether red or green. A design in which contrast of surface quality is the essential element might be equally successful carried out in one colour or in several colours.

The embroiderer has the means to construct infinite varieties of texture. Ridged, puckered and dimpled effects can be obtained by tucking, gathering, pleating and quilting fabrics. Other textures can be developed out of loosely woven fabric. Threads can be pulled and bound together to form a new texture or open-weave fabrics can be laced with different materials. With a variety of threads, all grades of texture can be made between the extremes of smooth and rough, and lines, knots and loops can be manipulated to achieve ribbed, grained and matted effects.

Spatial effects can be achieved with contrasts of texture. As a general rule, when the extremes of fine and coarse textures are contained in one design, the fine textures appear to recede into the background and coarse textures to advance. If we add to this the spatial effects of colour, light-dark and warm-cold contrasts, the sensation of space can be doubly enforced.

The question of correct balance and proportion of shape, colour and texture is complex and can only be discussed in terms of a particular design. It is, nonetheless, generally true to say that many different shapes, many colour and texture contrasts combined within one picture area leads to confused and aimless design.

(*above*) A highly textured surface is achieved by weaving narrow strips of contrasting fabrics into a background of drawn thread work (page 85). The background is slightly quilted with Terylene wadding (page 62), which is visible through areas where the threads have been removed. Closely related to the texture of fabric is the reflective quality of its surface. Rough, broken textures resulting from matt, slubbed or mixed yarns break up and absorb falling light, whereas smooth textures, such as satin, reflect light. Detail of a hanging by Julia Jeffries, 36 × 84 in. (914 × 2133 mm).

(*left*) A contrast of textures is created with frayed fabric, straight stitches, running stitch, and cretan stitch worked over running stitch. A rough texture can be effectively thrown into relief by contrasting it with a finer texture and light-dark, warm-cold colour contrasts used to enforce the sensation of space. Experimental embroidery by Julia Jeffries, 10 × 13 in. (255 × 330 mm).

PRELIMINARY DESIGN

The overall effect of an embroidery evolves out of the choice of theme and the materials and techniques used to execute it. It requires skill in designing and experience in manipulating materials to create a successful embroidery spontaneously; that is, without some previous consideration of the overall effect. To assess the eventual impact of an embroidery, many designers find it useful to make preliminary plans in other media, before beginning work in fabric and thread.

Plans and sketches can be made in any medium: cut paper, paint, pencil, chalk, crayons or wax pencils. If a preliminary design is worked out in fabric collage (to scale rather than to size), some of the textural contrast can be planned in the early stages. At first, it may be an advantage to experiment with several different arrangements of shapes and various colour schemes. This may lead to an interesting development of the original theme. Large designs can be planned to scale and at a later stage an outline drawing of the main shapes and area divisions made as a cartoon for transferring the design on to a background fabric. A tracing of the cartoon is useful in working designs of appliqué, as it can be used as a pattern for cutting shapes.

Since the character of each design is partially established by pattern and textural effects formed with threads and stitches, preliminary planning should include experiments working in these materials. At the planning stage, it is important to remember that stitches should lie close to the fabric if the article is to be worn or handled frequently. Threads can be left loose on the surface of the fabric if there is no danger of their being caught or pulled during handling, for example on panels and hangings.

A spontaneous design can be created out of the manipulation of material. Shapes can be cut out of fabric, thread stitched into patterns and textures, and both organized into a design, without reference to a previously determined scheme. At any stage in the development of such a design, new shapes, colours and textures may be introduced. This is an exciting way of working because, unless one has a clear 'mental picture', the outcome is totally unpredictable.

TOOLS AND EQUIPMENT

Paper

The cheapest paper, newsprint or lay-out (bank) paper, is adequate for preliminary roughs and sketches. Cartridge (construction), a thicker paper with a grained surface, is more suitable for colour studies. For planning areas of colour, coloured tissue paper is useful. Graph paper is excellent for planning geometric patterns and designs. Use tracing paper or grease-proof paper for transferring outlines of shape and pattern from paper to fabric. Drafting or cutting paper is available in plain white or ruled with squares. It is used for cutting patterns and can be useful for drawing out large-scale detailed designs. (It may also be used as a support in working machine embroidery with the presser foot removed, see page 115.)

Pencils

Keep several black lead pencils of different hardness to obtain the various effects you require. A hard pencil is useful for making clear, well-defined lines and can be used for working out small, precise designs and geometric patterns. There is a wide range of coloured pencils on the market today.

Charcoal, pastel, paint, etc.

Each of these has its own special quality which you may find sympathetic to your way of working. Drawings and preliminary studies can be worked in charcoal, wax or oil pastels and paint. Designers' gouache, coloured pastels and good quality felt-tip pens are all suitable for working studies in colour.

Other equipment

The following items are useful: drawing pins (thumb tacks), ruler, set square and protractor. A drawing board is a necessity if single sheets of paper are used, rather than sketching blocks or pads of paper.

TRANSLATING PRELIMINARY DESIGNS TO EMBROIDERY

Having worked out a design 'on paper', the appropriate materials and techniques must be chosen for its successful translation into embroidery.

When selecting materials, both texture and colour must be carefully considered. A small delicate design will lose some of its special quality if coarse fabrics are used. Transparent, open-weave, lace and net fabrics can be used to achieve merged shapes and colour effects. If it is not possible to buy the exact colour required, a fabric can be dyed or the colour scheme adjusted. Threads, too, must reflect the qualities of the preliminary design: finer threads are suitable for small delicate designs and thicker, heavier threads for large bold designs. Materials for functional items which will need washing or dry-cleaning should be chosen with those requirements in mind.

Selecting techniques may be difficult if there are several which seem equally appropriate. Some techniques, however, are obviously suited to certain kinds of designs. Clear-cut, well-defined shapes and patterns are effective in patchwork or appliqué or in wadded, stuffed or corded quilting. An alternative would be to use stitches, couching down threads or cords, or working line or straight stitches. Linear pattern could be worked in couched threads and cords, or in lines of stitching, which could be combined with areas of pleated and tucked fabric.

More fluid designs based on merged effects of shape and colour, translate well in appliqué, perhaps developed further with the addition of stitches, or stitchery alone might be chosen.

Stitchery is useful for translating textural qualities. Streaked effects and crosshatching can be interpreted by working the areas in varieties of running and straight stitches, in couched threads or by painting the areas with dye. Scribble and scratched effects can be interpreted in machine embroidery and grained effects obtainable with wax and oil crayons can be suggested with looped and knotted stitches.

2 Preparatory work

Many problems may be avoided by working in a logical, planned sequence and by following through the essential stages of preparatory work. The procedure outlined below may be helpful when working the first embroidery: it can be adapted and modified when some experience has been gained.

1 Make preliminary sketches and studies. Using paint, pencil or crayons, draw the design on paper showing the arrangement of shape and pattern. An alternative method is to cut out the shapes in paper (newspaper or tissue paper) and glue them to a background of paper. The paper shapes can be moved easily and the arrangement altered until a satisfactory design is achieved. Fabric could also be used in the initial planning stages (see page 20).

2 Draw the design to full scale. An outline of the main shapes and pattern only is necessary.

3 For embroidery worked on a frame, with the design transferred by the tacking method, first stretch the fabric on the frame and then transfer the design to it. If the design is transferred with carbon paper or fabric marker, first outline it on the top fabric then mount on to a backing and stretch on a frame.

4 Make patterns for all shapes to be applied in fabric.

5 Sew appliqué fabrics in position.

6 Work stitchery, beading, and add any other materials such as ribbons, braid, cord, etc.

7 When the embroidery is complete, neaten and present the work in any one of the ways suggested in the chapter 'Finishing and Presentation' (pages 122 to 130). In this chapter we shall consider preparatory work, stages 3 and 4.

TOOLS AND EQUIPMENT

Scissors

It is an advantage to have three pairs of scissors: one pair for cutting paper (patterns), a second pair for cutting fabric, these should be reasonably large and very sharp, and a third smaller pair with sharp points for cutting thread and small fabric shapes.

Embroidered panel by Carol Chorley, 24 × 24 in. (610 × 610 mm). Embroidery is a means of personal expression. Fabric and thread have been used here to interpret a theme based on personal imagery and imagination. A combination of techniques has been used: hand stitchery, applied padded areas and freehand painting.

(*right*) A rigid wooden frame suitable for working embroideries.
(*far right*) Strengthen large wooden frames with a central strut, and corner plates which can be cut from hardboard.

Tailors' chalk can be useful as it brushes away easily, but it will only last for a short time if the fabric is handled frequently. White and coloured tailors' chalks are available.

Frames

Many embroiderers find it easier to regulate the tension of stitches if the fabric is stretched taut over a frame. Generally the use of a frame will prevent the fabric from puckering unnecessarily during the stitching process.

Ring frames, often referred to as tambour frames, are used for working small designs. They consist of two rings of wood or metal which fit one inside the other, the outer ring having a tightening screw. They can be bought in various sizes from 3 to 12 in. (75 to 300 mm) in diameter.

Slate frames, square or rectangular embroidery frames, are fairly simple pieces of equipment. They can be used for pieces of work larger than about 10 in. (250 mm) square. A slate frame consists of two rollers with slits at either end and firmly attached webbing, and two slats or laths with holes at regular intervals. The slats fit into the slits of the rollers and are held in position with split pins or screws inserted into the holes. Frames can be bought in various sizes, the size being determined by the length of the webbing on the rollers.

Wooden frames or discarded picture frames can be used in place of ring or slate frames. Rigid wooden frames are relatively easy to make in any shape and size. The advantage of constructing them for oneself is that one is not limited to the scale of commercially manufactured frames. It is therefore possible to work on a very large scale if so desired.

Small frames can be made from 1 × 1 in. (25 × 25 mm) wood, larger frames from 1½ to 2 in. (38 to 50 mm) wood. Four pieces of wood are cut to the required length and held together with nails or screws, as illustrated. Very large frames should be made with a strengthening strut through the middle, to prevent distortion or warping when the fabric is stretched tightly over them. Fabric may be held temporarily with drawing pins (thumb tacks) while work is in progress.

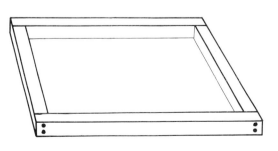
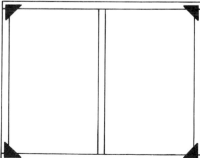

Discarded picture frames may be used for working embroidery if the wood is soft enough to take drawing pins. They should be cleaned thoroughly before use and, if the edges are rough or splintered, they should be bound with old cotton sheeting or calico.

Drawing pins (thumb tacks), staples and tacks

Good quality brass or steel drawing pins should be used for temporarily pinning fabric to wooden frames and for stretching completed embroidery. A staple gun (tacker) is useful for pinning completed embroidery to wooden stretchers. Metal tacks may be used in place of staples but they put more strain on the fabric and tend to damage it. They also have a tendency to rust.

Mounting board and cardboard

Cardboard can be used for stretching small embroideries. Choose a card which is thick enough not to buckle when the embroidery is stretched over it. Mounting card (matting board) is made in a range of colours, and is used for mounting small, previously stretched embroideries.

Miscellaneous items

A steel ruler with a cutting edge, a sharp Stanley knife (matt knife) and a metal plate or similar hard surface will be required for cutting card. A soft board (cork mat or insulating board) is useful for working mosaic and shell patchwork. The patches can be pinned in position on the board before sewing them together. An old drawing board or other soft wood surface is useful for damp-stretching embroidery (see page 122). A steel tape measure is easier to use than the cloth type. A thimble will prevent sore fingers.

BASIC WORKING STITCHES

Tacking (basting) stitch

This is a long running stitch (see page 88) used as a temporary means of holding fabrics together. It can also be used to transfer shapes and patterns to the fabric.

Stab stitch

This stitch is used to secure one fabric to the surface of another, for example, appliqué. The thread is brought up through the fabric and inserted close to where it first emerged, with the needle entering vertically each time. The thread passes over one or two threads of the fabric only.

Slip stitch

This stitch gives an invisible finish and is worked in a straight line along hems. It is used in blind appliqué (page 43). The thread is brought up first below the hem or folded edge of fabric with the needle inserted into the fold above its first emergence, coming out a short distance along the fold and the thread is pulled through. The needle then enters the fabric close to but just below the fold and emerges a short distance along; the thread is pulled through. The next stitch is worked into the folded edge. These movements are continued, working alternately through the fold and just below it.

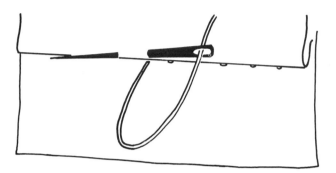

Oversewing (overcast stitch)

This stitch is worked from left to right and consists of small diagonal straight stitches. It can be worked over raw edges of fabric, to join fabric together as in mosaic patchwork. It may also be used in working pulled and drawn thread work, or as a purely decorative stitch.

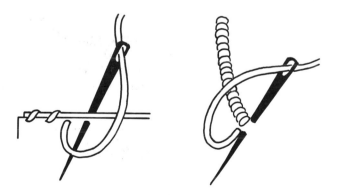

PREPARING FABRIC

Most fabrics require some ironing or pressing before they can be used. Always use the correct heat for the fabric in question. Those with a pile, such as velvet, corduroy and flannel, should be pressed lightly on the wrong side using a pressing cloth. A velvet board is ideal for pressing velvet and corduroy, but a thick, rough towel made into a pad can be used instead. Many fabrics fray quite easily and this can be prevented by oversewing by hand or machine, or binding the edges with tape before starting work. It is particularly important when not using a frame to protect the edges of very frayable fabric used as a background for embroidery.

BACKING A FABRIC

A foundation or backing fabric of calico (muslin) or cotton sheeting will be required for working log cabin and crazy patchwork, and for embroidery to be carried out with a combination of different weights of fabric. Embroidery worked on lightweight fabrics is more successful if bleached calico, cotton lawn, or cotton sheeting is used as a backing. A medium- or heavyweight calico is suitable for most purposes.

To mount a piece of fabric on to a backing, cut both top and backing fabric to equal size and shape. Allow at least $1\frac{1}{2}$ in. (38 mm) extra on each side of the design for turning and neatening the edges when work is complete. Bind or oversew all edges which are likely to fray. Place the top fabric with right side facing upwards on the backing fabric and pin. All edges should meet exactly, and the grain of both fabrics should be square (see page 38). Tack or baste the two fabrics together with vertical and horizontal lines, starting in the centre and working outwards to the edges. Make sure both fabrics are smooth and unwrinkled while tacking. If you are mounting a large piece of fabric, tack further lines at intervals across and down the length of the shape, always beginning at a point along the first vertical and horizontal lines. Lines of tacking 4 to 6 in. (100 to 150 mm) apart will ensure that the fabrics remain smooth and unwrinkled while work is in progress.

A different procedure is called for if the embroidery is to be stretched on a frame. The methods for each type of frame are described below.

MOUNTING FABRIC ON FRAMES

Dressing a frame is the technical term given to the process of mounting fabric on to a frame.

To dress a ring frame (for a small embroidery) first cut the fabric to about 2 to 3 in. (50 to 75 mm) larger than the diameter of the frame. Place the inner ring on a flat surface and cover with the fabric. Position the outer ring over the fabric and inner ring and push down gently. Tighten the screw slightly. Make sure the fabric is taut and free from wrinkles and the grain is straight (see page 38). Then tighten the screw until it is firmly gripped. To prevent delicate fabrics being marked by wooden frames, bind the inner ring with strips of soft fabric (lawn, for example) or with smooth tape. A bound frame will also grip slippery fabrics such as satin.

The process of mounting fabric on to a slate frame can be divided into two main stages.

1 Preparing the fabric. Cut a rectangle of fabric on the straight of the grain. The width should not be greater than that of the webbing on the rollers and the length can be longer than the length of the fully extended frame (length is determined by the slats with holes). Tack or baste horizontal and vertical lines of stitching through the centre of the fabric. Fold under a $\frac{1}{2}$ in. (13 mm) turning on both top and bottom edges of the fabric and tack or baste (at a later stage these edges are sewn to the webbing, see below). The sides of the piece must be strengthened to take the strain of lacing which is carried out at a later

Slate frame
A Rollers with slits and attached webbing
B Slats
C Tape
D Lacing: string or carpet thread
E Backing fabric
F Top fabric

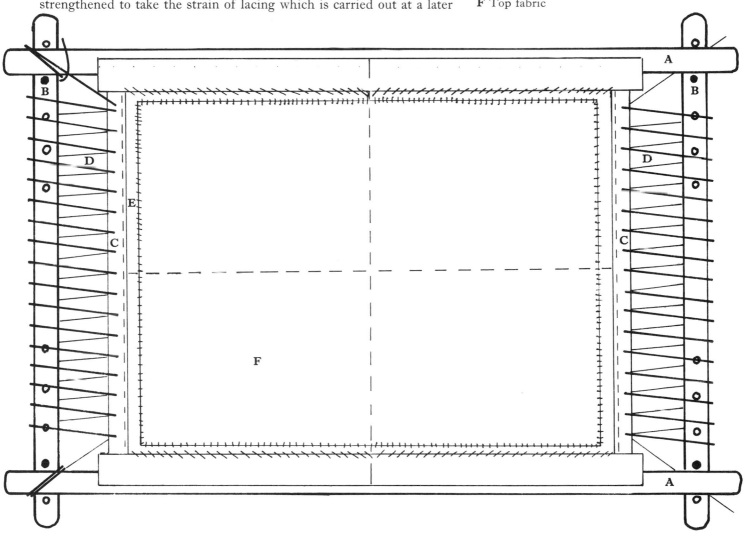

stage. If the fabric is firm and closely woven, strengthen both edges by turning and tacking $\frac{1}{2}$ in. (13 mm) of fabric down over a piece of string. In this way the string is encased in the turning. If an open-weave fabric is used or the fabric is liable to fray badly (canvas or even-weave linen, for example) the sides must be bound with tape to make a firm strong edge. Pin and tack the tape in position and stitch firmly with straight machine stitch or back stitch using a strong cotton thread.

2 Mounting fabric on to the frame. Mark the centre of the webbing on the two rollers. Place the centre of the top edge of the fabric to the top centre of the webbing. Pin in position, working from the centre outwards and with the pins at right angles to the edge. Tack firmly and remove pins. Using a strong thread (buttonhole twist) stitch the fabric to the webbing with a close, even overcast stitch. Stitch from the centre outwards to one side, then to the other side. Repeat this process on the bottom roller. If the length of the piece of fabric is longer than the length of the fully extended frame, roll the extra fabric around one of the rollers. Slip the slats (side arms) into the slits in the rollers. The four sides of the frame are fixed in position by inserting the split pins or screws in the appropriate holes. The fabric should be pulled taut but not too tight. The side edges of the fabric are laced over the slats using a strong thread (carpet thread or string) and a large needle (a heavy embroidery needle would be suitable). Work from the centre of the side and lace the thread over the slat and through the edge of the fabric (whether this is encased string or taped) at intervals of about 1 in. (25 mm). Allow a sufficient length of string for tying to the ends of the frame. The fabric may slacken while work is in progress but an even tension can be maintained by tightening the lacing strings.

Most fabrics will give better results if worked with backing fabric beneath them. To secure backing and top fabric to a slate frame, first mount the backing as outlined above. Then cut the top fabric to size and place it, with the right side facing upwards, on the mounted backing. Pin and then tack vertical and horizontal lines through the centre of the fabrics. Begin each line in the centre of the shape and work towards the edges, smoothing the top fabric outwards. Sew the edges of the top fabric to the backing with small straight stitches worked over, and at right angles to, the edges. Stitch from the middle of each side outwards towards the corners.

Wooden frames similar to those used by painters are ideal stretchers for large embroidery. They are not difficult to construct (see page 27). To stretch fabric on such a frame, cut a square or rectangle 3 to 4 in. (75 to 100 mm) larger than the frame. (The fabric should be cut and pinned on the straight grain.) Mark the centre of each side of both the fabric and frame. Pin, using drawing pins (thumb tacks), the centre of each side of the fabric to the centre of each side of the frame, pulling the fabric taut. N.B. Pins must go into the side of the frame not the top. Continue pinning, working from the centre of each side outwards to the corners. The fabric should be pulled taut but not so tight that the threads are pulled out of line. If backing fabric as well as background fabric is to be used, first pin the backing as described above and then pin the top fabric. Leave the drawing pins in place while working and if the fabric slackens remove them one at a time and pull the fabric tight again.

When work is complete the fabric can be held permanently on the frame with staples or tacks. In some embroideries, applied fabric and stitched areas may have to be worked right to the edges of the total design. Since it is difficult to sew where the fabric runs over the upper surfaces of the wooden frame, it is better to work on a larger frame and transfer the finished work to a smaller one.

TRANSFERRING DESIGNS ON TO FABRIC

The success of the final piece of work depends, to some extent, on the way in which the original design is transferred to fabric. If this design has been made on paper, there are several methods of transferring it. Whichever method is chosen, only the main areas of division, shape and pattern need be marked on the fabric. These marks should provide an adequate guide for the correct working of the embroidery. Subdivisions of shape can be marked if it is felt that they will assist in the working of embroidery.

Tracing and tacking (basting)
This is one of the simplest and most accurate methods of transferring a design. Draw the design to full size, and take a tracing. Tissue paper is suitable for tracing small designs, tracing paper for larger designs. Tack or baste the tracing to the fabric and outline the design with running or tacking stitch worked through both paper and fabric. Use tacking thread for the stitching. Then tear the paper away leaving the design outlined in stitches on the fabric. This method may be used in preparing fabric to be worked on a frame. Stretch the fabric on the frame and then tack the design on to the fabric. It may also be used for marking the design on unstretched fabric, for example, hangings and banners worked without the use of a frame. It is the best method for marking coarse and heavy textured fabrics.

Transfer inks and pencils
The method is only suitable for designs where fabric or threads and stitches will completely cover the inked lines. It is more successful

on smooth closely woven fabric. Draw out the design to full size, place tracing paper over it and mark the outlines of shape and pattern with either transfer ink or pencil. Use the tracing like a printed transfer: turn it over on to the fabric and iron to the material. This method gives a mirror image of the design. To obtain exactly the same design as drawn on paper, two tracings will have to be taken. Take the first tracing from the drawing, using ink or felt tip pen, which should be waterproof to avoid smudging. Then turn it over and take a second tracing, this time using the transfer pencil or ink.

Carbon paper

Special embroidery carbon paper is available in blue, red and yellow. Place the carbon paper face down on the fabric with the drawing over it facing upwards. Draw over the outlines of the design with pencil or a tracing wheel, using sufficient pressure to leave an impression on the fabric. The best results are obtained if the fabric is stretched and pinned firmly to a drawing board. This method is not strongly recommended, however, as the carbon paper is apt to smudge.

Pouncing

This is the most elaborate method of transferring a design to fabric. Place a tracing of the design over a layer of felt or blanket and pin both to a board. Then pierce the outline of the design through. A special pin mounted on a handle can be obtained, but a thick pin can be used just as successfully. The holes should be close together. When the piercing is complete remove the tracing. The rough edges of the holes, which otherwise might close up, should be rubbed down with fine sandpaper (glasspaper). Then pin the fabric to a drawing board or similar surface and with drawing pins attach the pierced tracing, right side up, to the fabric. Rub the lines of holes firmly with a pad of soft fabric coated with powdered charcoal or chalk. Use french chalk for marking dark-toned fabrics and a mixture of charcoal and chalk for light-toned. The pressure must be firm to force the powder through the holes. Remove the paper carefully and gently blow the surplus powder away. Join up the lines of dots and fix them to the fabric with watercolour paint or designers' gouache. Use a colour which will show up on the fabric. The paint should be reasonably thick, so that it does not run or bleed out from the lines. This method is useful when working small designs and those which involve much intricate stitchery.

Fabric markers

Dressmakers' pencils, which are available in several colours, can be used for drawing freehand designs. Pin the fabric to a board and draw the design with the pencil. Since some of these colours are permanent it is advisable to make a test piece to ensure that the marks can be removed from the fabric with a damp sponge. Tailors' chalk may be used for drawing temporary lines directly on to the fabric.

Paper patterns and templates

Appliqué will be more accurate if paper patterns are cut for all the shapes to be applied. To make these patterns, draw the design in outline to the correct scale, then trace off each shape indicating by arrows the straight of the grain. It is best to leave plenty of space round each tracing in case a turning allowance is required.

Templates are master shapes from which paper patterns are cut for working mosaic and shell patchwork. They are produced commercially in most geometric shapes and a variety of sizes. Templates are usually sold in pairs, one 'solid' shape and one 'window' shape (see page 47).

3 Fabric and thread

In this chapter we shall consider the nature and qualities of fabric and threads and how their construction affects the ways in which they can be used.

FABRIC

There is a wide range of fabrics on the market today and both natural and synthetic fibres are used in their construction, either alone or in various combinations. Almost any of these fabrics can be used in embroidery, some responding more readily than others to particular methods and techniques. Knowledge and experience of how they respond to particular treatments can be gained by experimenting with various fabrics before actually using them in a particular piece of work. Working experimental samplers may reveal new and subtle effects that can be added to the designer's store of information for future reference.

Textural qualities are inherent in a fabric and cannot be disregarded when planning and working embroidery. The texture results from the type of yarn or thread used, and the way it is constructed. Since yarn can be woven, knitted or pressed in various ways, the resulting fabrics are extremely varied. The structure of woven fabrics can be changed to produce a range of close, plain weaves such as taffeta, calico (muslin) and plain cotton, open-weave fabrics such as voile and organdie, and closely woven twilled fabrics, surah, either silk or rayon, and serge. Knitted fabrics of cotton, wool, silk, or synthetic fibres can be obtained in various weights. One of the well-known pressed fabrics is felt, produced by exerting extreme pressure on fibres of wool or hair. Yarns used in fabric construction are extremely varied and include natural fibres, silk, cotton, wool and linen, even jute, sisal, hair and grasses, and synthetic yarns of rayon, nylon, Terylene, plastic, tricel, polyester and many others. These yarns are spun and produced in a variety of thicknesses, so that while fabrics may be made of the same basic materials, they differ in their structure, weight and texture. For example, there is a wide variety of silk fabrics ranging from fine, almost transparent organdie and chiffon, to more closely woven opaque types, such as taffeta, surah, 'Jap' (or lining) silk, shantung, lightweight wild silk, the more obviously textured hand-woven Indian silk, and silk voile. In some instances the yarn is spun with varying thicknesses along its length and when woven or knitted, this produces a fabric with a slubbed or knobbly texture, as in tweeds of wool or synthetic threads, rough linen and some calico. Fabrics of wool and of cotton are manufactured in as great a variety as silk, and are available in fine or thick, close or open, smooth or rough weaves. The surface of some fabrics is brushed to produce a fine pile or down (wool, velour, flannel, brushed rayon and rayon). Other fabrics of animal hair, such as lambswool, mohair, camel-hair, are available either smooth or thicker with a more pronounced hairy texture. Cotton varieties include closely woven and smooth fabrics (lawn, cambric, sateen), fine more open-weave fabrics (organdie, voile), rough-spun unbleached calico, twill, gaberdine, denim, knitted cotton, towelling, velveteen and corduroy.

Closely related to the texture of a fabric is the reflective quality of the surface: some have a noticeable sheen. The degree of reflection depends upon the evenness of the weave, and the smoothness of the surface. Rough, broken textures, resulting from matt, slubbed or mixed yarns break up and absorb falling light.

Satin is an obvious example of a fabric with a highly reflective surface; others include polished rayon, often of the knitted variety, glitter nylon, and P.V.C. (sheet plastic). Furnishing fabrics, in many instances suitable for embroidery, are produced with varying degrees of sheen. Frequently the right side of the fabric is shiny and the reverse side is matt; their contrasting reflective qualities could be emphasized by using both sides in the same design. Shiny and matt threads are used in conjunction for the construction of some fabrics, giving a broken, glittery effect (wool and lurex, lurex-cotton). Woollen fabric is usually matt, although woollen facecloth has quite a smooth surface with a slight sheen. The range and subtleties of these surfaces are many and can be exploited particularly well with patchwork and appliqué.

Further factors to be considered when choosing fabrics are flexibility and weight, for these will determine their use in embroidery. Soft, fine fabrics of silk, wool, cotton and synthetics are usually quite flexible and can be gathered, pleated, tucked, smocked and folded, either with the grain or against it. All fine fabrics and open-weave fabrics can be used for appliqué. While some can be used for cutwork and patchwork, more satisfactory results will be obtained with firmer, more closely woven fabrics which have more body and are less likely to fray. Soft, light- and medium-weight fabrics can be successfully padded, quilted and stuffed, as can knitted and stretch fabrics. Medium-weight fabrics, wool, velvet, corduroy, thick cotton, synthetics and many soft furnishings can also be satisfactorily folded and pleated and are ideal for appliqué. Velvets, when folded, produce exceptionally good results as light falling on the pile gives interesting tonal changes. Corduroy also produces tonal changes if the fabric is cut and put together with the grain going in different directions. Heavy fabrics, thick tweeds and hessian (burlap), are generally more suitable for appliqué and for use as background fabrics. Stiff, tough fabrics are difficult to sew through and should be avoided if a considerable amount of hand embroidery is involved. For drawn and pulled thread work, a loose or open-weave fabric, whether linen, woollen or synthetic, is most suitable. Scrim is quite good for use with experimental drawn and pulled thread work, and also for free machine embroidery. Synthetic fabrics, plastics, P.V.C. and polythene, can also produce interesting results. The thin plastic types can be used in a similar way to fabrics of natural fibres but, unlike thicker plastics, they need a cotton backing to avoid splitting. Unbacked plastic cannot be unpicked if mistakes are made when working.

Grain of fabric

Woven fabric consists of two series of threads referred to as warp and weft threads. The warp threads run the length of the fabric and the weft threads interlace across the width of the fabric. The grain of a fabric is represented by these threads. In 'true' woven fabric warp and weft threads interlace at right angles and, if correctly made, the grain and structure are square with each other.

THREADS

The invention of and recent improvements in synthetic fibres and yarns have added an enormous range of threads to the existing selection made of natural fibres.

Threads produced for embroidery are generally made from natural substances: cotton, silk, wool and linen. Cotton varieties are made with a polished surface (stranded cotton, coton perlé or pearl cotton, coton-à-broder or embroidery cotton) or a matt surface (soft cotton). They are available in a wide range of colours and are usually sold in small skeins. Stranded cotton skeins normally consist of six strands. The strands can be separated, and any number of strands can be threaded through a needle. Coton perlé, a tightly twisted thread, is available in small skeins and balls, and a variety of different thicknesses. Silk threads are more difficult to obtain, and the selection is limited. Six-stranded embroidery silk and twisted silk embroidery threads are available. Two kinds of wool threads or yarns, crewel and tapestry, are produced for embroidery. Crewel wool is a fine 2-ply yarn that can be used singly or a number of threads can be threaded through a needle. Tapestry wool is a thicker 4-ply wool. Linen thread can be obtained but, as with silk, the range is limited.

The warp threads run the length of the fabric and the weft threads interlace across the width of the fabric.

Threads, yarns and twines produced for purposes other than embroidery can be an effective way of adding variety and interest to designs. There is a wide range of wool and synthetic knitting yarns, chenille and courtelle, for example. Lurex (synthetic) and lurex mixtures could also be useful. Gold-fingering, an untarnishable gold-coloured thread, which is also available in silver and copper colours, may effectively be worked into an embroidery. Rug wool, available in different thicknesses, has a pleasant matt surface and could be used in contrast with more shiny threads. Wool thrums, ends cut from the loom when weaving is complete, can be obtained from carpet manufacturers. It is usually sold in hanks of medium and long strands. There are a number of different gold and silver threads, passing, bullion, purl and plate, and synthetic substitutes for metal threads are available. Several types of crochet and macramé yarns (wool and cotton), natural and synthetic string, raffia and twine could be added to the list. Yarn unravelled from woven fabric is a further source of threads.

Threads for machine embroidery are available in two thicknesses No. 30 and No. 50. No. 30 is the thicker of the two and produces a more definite stitched effect. Some machine sewing cottons can be used for decorative stitching and free embroidery on the machine. Trident and Sericum mercerized cotton is produced in a good range of colours. No. 60 mercerized cotton is similar in thickness to No. 30 machine embroidery cotton. A synthetic metal thread is produced for machine embroidery.

Ordinary sewing thread has its uses in embroidery; it is used in the making of patchwork and appliqué. Nos. 40, 60, 80 and 100 should suit most fabrics. Silk sewing thread and buttonhole thread would be useful. Buttonhole thread gives pleasing results when working small fine decorative stitches.

4 Fabric techniques I:
applied and flat surfaces

APPLIQUÉ

Appliqué (or applied work) is the technique of gluing (collage) or sewing one fabric on top of another. Contrasts and harmonies of patterned and plain, textures and colour can be exploited in this way. The technique is particularly suitable for use in panels or hangings, as it enables the designer to combine fabrics of different qualities in one design. Glued appliqué is suitable only if the finished work will not require washing.

1 Select a background fabric. Where the background plays an important part in the design, its colour, texture and pattern should enhance the applied shapes. If the whole area is to be covered by appliqué, either calico (muslin) or medium-weight plain cotton is adequate as a support.

2 If the design is intricate, make paper patterns for all the shapes (see page 35) and pin them to the right side of the fabric to be applied. Make sure the grain of the applied fabrics will be straight with the grain of the background material. If the grains do not match, the appliqué is liable to pull and drag out of line. Draw round each pattern with tailors' chalk or a fabric marker. If tailors' chalk is used, tack or baste along each drawn line. Where no preliminary detailed design has been worked out, shapes can be cut and glued or sewn in a spontaneous arrangement.

3 Where the shapes are to be left with raw edges, cut out on the exact outline of each shape. Applied shapes with sharp points are best used with raw edges, as turning the edges under is difficult, especially when the points are small; with thick fabrics and those that fray easily, turned edges can be messy.

For applied shapes with a turned edge, tack or baste the outline of the shape on to the fabric and cut out $\frac{1}{2}$ in. (13 mm) from the edge. Leave a larger surplus for turning if the fabric frays easily; if necessary this may be trimmed back at a later stage.

4 Use an interlining where the fabric requires added weight and stiffness or for fine fabrics which are to be kept flat and firm, or for stretchable fabrics. Vilene (Pellon) or lightweight calico or cotton are suitable. Iron-on-Vilene is adequate for use with raw-edged shapes. Cut the interlining to the exact size of the appliqué shape, using a paper pattern where necessary, and tack or iron it on to the reverse side of the material.

5 Remove any patterns that may have been used.

Embroidered panel by Danena Wrightson Hunt, 13 × 8 in. (330 × 203 mm). Both stitched and glued appliqué have been used in this small panel in which a pattern of stripes executed in machine stitch is contrasted with the scribble effects of frayed edges and loops of wool and felt. Appliqué need not be flat. Fabric can be squashed into interesting shapes and textures, and any materials combined to achieve an infinite variety of effects.

40

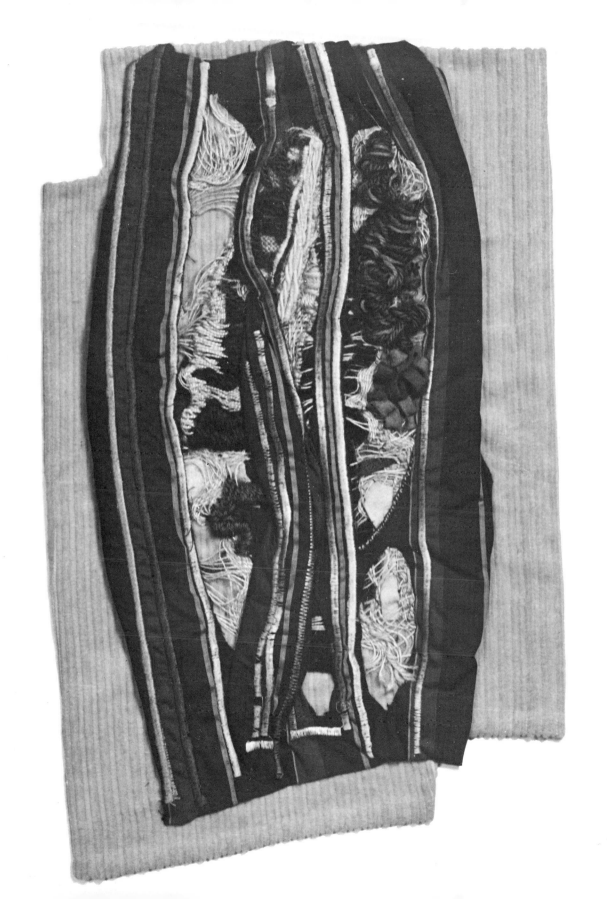

6 For turned or hemmed edges, turn the surplus material under to the wrong side and to the precise edge of the shape. Tack firmly. If the shape has a convex curve, pleat the fullness into the hem. For concave curves, make snips in the turning allowance at right angles to the edge.

Glued appliqué

This method is generally more successful with raw-edged shapes. Spread the wrong side of the cut shape with a fabric adhesive and press into position on the ground fabric. Allow it to dry completely before attempting any stitching. In some instances the adhesive can alter the surface quality or make a fabric too stiff, so it is advisable to make a test sample before using it for the embroidery design. This applies particularly to fine or loosely woven fabrics. Gluing is more effective with thick or closely woven fabrics such as felt, cotton, P.V.C. (sheet plastic) and leather.

Fabrics need not always be glued completely smooth and flat: one part of the shape only could be glued down, perhaps in the middle, leaving the surrounding part loose. Fabric can be cut larger than the area to be covered, then squashed and eased up into the required shape, giving interesting textural results.

Stitched appliqué

Follow the appropriate preliminary stages 1 to 6, then position the appliqué shapes on the ground fabric, and pin and tack firmly in place. (This applies to appliqué with either a raw edge or a turned edge.) Secure them finally with either hand or machine stitching.

There are several simple methods of sewing raw edges in place. Straight stitches (page 94) worked at right angles to the edge and $\frac{1}{8}$ to $\frac{1}{4}$ in. (3 to 6 mm) apart is one of the easiest. The stitches can be worked farther apart on larger, simple shapes. Work the stitch by bringing the needle from the back through both the ground fabric and the appliqué a short distance inside the edge of the shape. Then take the needle and thread down close to the edge of the shape, but through the ground fabric only. This method works particularly well with frayable fabrics, and makes for an easy flow between the background and the appliqué. Stab stitch (page 28) is another useful stitch for a simple unobtrusive effect. Running and back stitches (pages 88 and 92) or straight and zigzag machine stitches can be used, working them close to the edge of the appliqué, but they will emphasize the edge to some degree. Satin stitch (page 94), either hand or machine, will give a hard effect, isolating the shape of the appliqué. Threads should be chosen to suit the fabrics. No. 40 sewing cotton and silk are adequate for medium-weight materials, a finer sewing cotton, Nos. 60 or 100, is used for fine fabrics, and buttonhole thread for thicker and heavier fabrics. Unless the method of securing the appliqué is part of the overall design it is best to use a thread of the same colour as the appliqué.

In blind appliqué, the edge of the shape is turned under (hemmed) and then sewn into place with a slip stitch (page 29). A normal sewing thread is used in a matching colour and none of the stitches should show. This method can be applied where a clear edge between the shape and the ground is required. Other stitches for turned edges include back or running stitches or a machine straight stitch; these are worked close to the edge of the appliqué. Although the treatment of the turned edge is similar to that of the raw edge, the effect is quite different, having a more even, smooth quality. However closely woven a fabric is, a raw edge always frays a little, producing an uneven quality.

SEAMS

For many embroidery designs seaming fabrics together is not necessary. An appliqué method is more suitable for working flat designs (panels and hangings) consisting of complex shapes and many different fabrics. However, seaming may be useful for joining simple shapes and for joining different fabrics which are then to be pleated, tucked, gathered, draped, etc. It allows for changes of colour and pattern without the added weight or stiffness that would result from an appliqué method. Seams are obviously required for the construction of three-dimensional forms (page 72).

Various dressmaking seams can be adapted for creative embroidery. For working areas of stitchery over joined fabrics flat or lapped seaming is suitable. In flat seams no stitching is apparent but the stitching for a lapped seam is worked on the surface. More detailed methods of seaming can be incorporated into the pattern and design. The flattish ridge of the french seam, for example, could be used to good effect on the right side of the work.

Stitching can be worked on a machine, using a straight stitch of correct size for the weight and structure of the fabric. If a machine is not available, back stitch can be substituted. A normal sewing thread (cotton, silk, or synthetic) is suitable for most fabrics. Use No. 40 for thick fabrics and No. 50 or No. 60 for fine fabrics.

Flat seam
Bring the two edges of the fabric together with the right sides facing each other, and tack or baste. Make the seam by working a line of straight stitching (machine or back stitch) about ½ in. (13 mm) from the edges of the fabric. Press the seam allowance open to achieve a smooth flat seam.

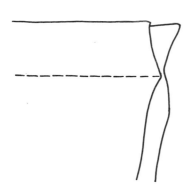

Lapped seam

A normal lapped seam is worked in the following way. Turn the seam allowance of one edge under to the wrong side of the fabric and tack. Then place the edge over the seam allowance of the other fabric with the fold meeting the seam line. Tack. Work straight stitching close to the folded edge or a short distance from it. A piped effect can be given by threading cord or string through the channel made by working the stitched line away from the folded edge.

Raw edges produce pleasing effects in the right context and lapped seams can be worked in this way. Instead of turning the seam allowance under, place it flat over the edge of the other fabric, and stitch in place as described above. Several rows of stitching could be worked, giving added strength and decorative qualities.

Channel seam

Fabrics joined by this method are not sewn together; they are sewn to an underlay. Turn the seam allowance on both edges under to the wrong side of the fabric and tack. Place the folded edges on either side on top of the strip of underlay fabric and tack. Finally stitch in position with machine straight stitch, zigzag, or back stitch. This seam can be used to join different fabrics and as a background for a stitched design. It is useful for making up three-dimensional padded forms.

French seam

Bring the edges of the fabric together with wrong sides facing. Work a stitched line down the middle of the seam allowance, which can be trimmed slightly for a narrow seam. Then fold the fabric to the wrong side, and work a further line of stitching parallel to the edge and far enough away from it to encase the raw edges. A french seam is not only a neat way of joining two fabrics together – the flat ridge can be worked into the design of the embroidery. Start with the right sides of the fabric together and stitch and trim as described above; then turn the fabric to the right side and stitch in the normal way.

PATCHWORK

Patchwork is a technique in which fabric scraps are assembled and sewn together to construct a whole fabric.

From humble beginnings, rooted in economic necessity, patchwork has developed into a rich and often elaborate form of decoration. The technique can be divided into four main categories, determined by the shapes and method of construction involved. Mosaic patchwork generally consists of geometric shapes (squares, diamonds, hexagons, etc.) which are sewn together edge to edge. The patterns may be made using one shape only but two or more shapes may be combined. In shell patchwork the patches are overlapped and hemmed together on the right side of the work. The finished effect consists of overlapped circles. Unlike mosaic and shell patchwork, the two following methods require a foundation fabric, and in this are akin to applied work. Crazy patchwork consists of patches of any shape and size sewn to a foundation. Log cabin patchwork consists of strips of fabric sewn to a foundation. Traditionally the strips were arranged either around four sides of a square and filling it or diagonally across narrow lengths of a foundation fabric. The units (squares or narrow lengths) were joined to form the complete article.

Planning patchwork

When designing a patchwork it is worth remembering the effects that can be achieved by contrasting dark and light colours and combinations of patterned and plain fabrics. Printed and woven patterns in the fabric can effectively emphasize parts of the design. Tonal qualities give variety to flat pattern and can be successfully manipulated to produce illusions of three dimensions.

The first steps in planning a patchwork can be made by collecting scraps and oddments of fabrics with a colour scheme in mind. It is advisable to assemble enough to complete the article before starting the work. The collection can, if necessary, be supplemented by bought fabrics, but 'true' patchwork relies on the use of oddments. When working crazy patchwork no preliminary planning is necessary, for it is essentially a spontaneous and random technique. More detailed planning is necessary for working mosaic, shell, or log cabin patchwork. The design can initially be drawn on paper, working out the arrangement of shapes and placing tone values. It is not necessary for the designs to be drawn out to full size. A scaled down plan is quite adequate if it shows the relationship of shapes and tones. For this purpose squared graph paper or drafting paper is a useful aid to accuracy.

Planning is essential when designing mosaic patchworks consisting of several geometric shapes of different sizes, for it is important to know how the various shapes fit together. Designs for shell or log cabin patchwork are based on one shape only. Some of the best effects in these types of patchwork are gained through a play and contrast of colour and tone.

Fabrics

Fabrics of different yarns and textures, wool, cotton, linen and synthetics can be mixed (if the patchwork will require washing, fabrics should be chosen accordingly). Various effects are achieved from

Mosaic patchwork generally consists of geometric shapes which are sewn together edge to edge. A combination of plain and patterned hexagonals and triangles have been used in this design. The variations of tone give a three-dimensional effect – the lighter plain colours appearing to advance from the darker background – and an illusion of circular movement. Patchwork by Sue Moss, 20 × 20 in. (510 × 510 mm).

contrasting shiny and matt surfaces, for example, velvet and silk, wool and cotton, satin and corduroy. Different fabrics can be freely mixed for log cabin and crazy patchwork, but a foundation fabric will be required to prevent patches of heavier fabric pulling or dragging on lighter patches. The foundation material should be firm and medium weight; calico (muslin) or cotton sheeting is adequate.

Fabric for mosaic and shell patchwork requires more careful selection: equal weights are essential if the surface is to be kept smooth and flat. Mixing different weights of fabric could cause dragging, and fine fabrics could be pulled out of shape by patches of heavy fabrics. Although most weights of fabric can be used for mosaic and shell patchwork, try to avoid using thick fabric when making small patches. Many varieties of furnishing and dress cotton, silk, wool and synthetics are suitable for these types of patchwork, so long as they do not fray badly when cut.

Equipment and materials

Templates are required for making mosaic and shell patchwork. Made in metal or plastic, they can be bought in various shapes and sizes, and are normally sold in pairs, one 'solid' shape and one 'window' shape. The solid shape is the size of the finished patch with turnings and the one from which the paper patterns are cut. The window shape is used for marking out the shapes on the fabric. Templates can be made at home from stiff card, thin perspex (Plexiglass) or metal. Card can be cut easily with a Stanley (matt) knife, perspex with a fine hacksaw and thin metals (tin or copper) with metal shears. The templates, particularly the smaller one, must be drawn accurately and cut precisely. Inaccurate templates result in ill-fitting patchwork. Home-made templates allow more opportunity for experimenting with new shapes and provide a greater selection of sizes, but those made of card will normally last for one piece of work only.

A firm but flexible paper is required for cutting the patterns. It must be firm so that the fabric can be folded over crisply without distorting the edge of the pattern, and flexible enough to fold with the fabric during the working process. A reasonable quality writing paper or thin cartridge (construction) paper is suitable.

Normal cotton sewing thread is suitable for most fabrics, although fine silk should be sewn with silk thread. Linen, wool, cotton velvet and satin may be sewn with cotton thread. The thread should be fairly fine, as the joining stitches need to be small and closely worked, Nos. 60, 80 or 100 will suit most fabrics. The colour of the thread should tone with the colours of the fabric: white or light-toned thread for light-toned fabric and black or dark-toned thread for dark-toned patches.

Fine needles will aid the working of small close stitching necessary for a strong flat seam. Either sharps or betweens may be used: sizes 9 and 10 are generally suitable.

Mosaic patchwork

The method described here for making and joining hexagonal patches is used for all geometric straight-sided shapes: rectangles, squares, diamonds, octagons, etc. The same process is also used for making patchwork of different sizes of irregular straight-sided shapes. Before making a patchwork of irregular shapes, cut paper patterns for each shape and check that they all fit together. These patterns are used in stages **1** and **2** of the following working method.

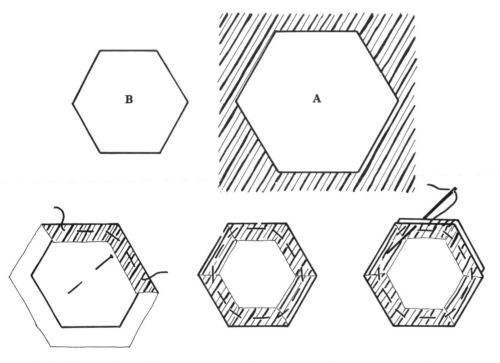

1 Cut a number of paper patterns from the solid template, B. The shape may be outlined with pencil but care must be taken to ensure that they are identical.

2 Cut fabric patches from the window template, A. The outline of the shape may be marked with a fabric marker on the wrong side of the fabric.

3 Pin the paper pattern on the wrong side and in the centre of the fabric patch.

4 Turn the seam allowance down over the paper pattern and tack or baste.

5 When a number of patches have been prepared, join them in the following way. Place the right sides of the patches together and work

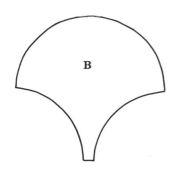

oversewing stitch (page 29) over the edges of the patches. Stitch close to the folded edge, avoiding the paper pattern. The stitches should be close and even but not so tight that the fabric is split or pulled. When constructing a large area of patchwork it may be easier to join patches into groups or units, and finally join the units to complete the work.

6 When all the patches are joined, lightly press the seams on the wrong side of the work. Remove the tacking and paper patterns.

Shell patchwork

1 Using a thin card (postcard) or thick paper, cut a number of patterns using template B. A sharp pencil may be used to outline the shape.

2 Cut a number of fabric patches using template A.

3 Pin the card pattern to the right side of the fabric patch.

4 Tack the seam allowance of the convex curve only down on the wrong side of the fabric patch, working the stitches through the fabric only and using the card pattern as a guide. The fullness in the seam allowance should be neatly pleated. The concave curves are left flat, and provide the surface to which the next row of patches is stitched.

5 Remove the pins and patterns.

6 The patches are joined on the right side of the work. Lay the first row of patches with right sides upwards and the edges just touching. The next row of patches is laid with the convex curves overlapping the hems of the first. The centre of each patch in the second row and each subsequent row is positioned where two patches in the preceding row meet. Pin together and tack, working along the curved edges and through the hems.

7 Work hemming stitch, slip stitch (page 29) or machine straight stitch round the semi-circular edge of each patch. The stitching is worked on the right side of the work and should be close and even.

8 Remove tacking and press lightly on the wrong side of the work.

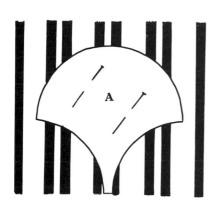

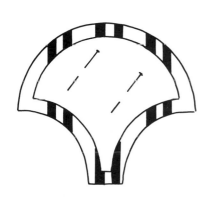

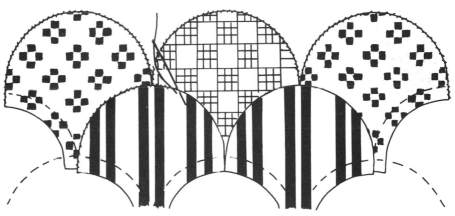

Crazy patchwork

No previously prepared design is needed for this as fabric patches are cut and arranged during the working process. A foundation fabric of cotton sheeting or calico (muslin) is required and a selection of off-cuts and scraps of fabric.

1 Cut a piece of foundation fabric to the required size and shape.

2 Trim the fabric, cutting away badly frayed areas and sharp or very irregular ends.

3 Pin the first patch to the foundation fabric. Add the next patch, overlapping the first by about ½ in. (13 mm).

4 Each patch can be stitched to the foundation before the next patch is added or, alternatively, all the patches can be pinned and tacked in place before final stitching takes place. Back stitch (page 92) or running stitch (page 88) may be used for hand-stitched crazy patchwork. For machine-stitched work, straight stitch or zigzag may be used. A line of close zigzag (satin stitch) worked over the raw edges of the patches will give a neatened and more definite edge.

Detail of a hanging by Julia Jeffries, 21 × 48 in. (534 × 1220 mm). Hessian is both applied and used as a background for machine and hand stitches worked in stranded cotton and coton perlé (pearl cotton) threads. The interest has been achieved by contrasting an ordered pattern of stripes and checks with areas of frayed hessian. Colour is often associated with physical and emotional sensations – warm, cold, dreary, happy. The use of warm colour for the cat helps to suggest a lively but contented animal.

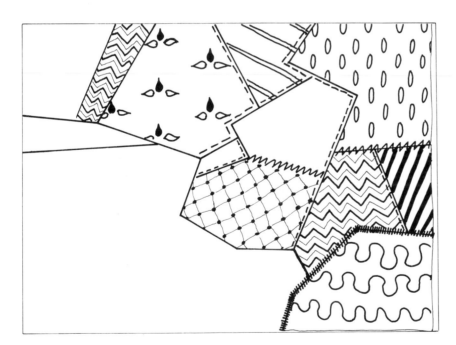

Log cabin patchwork

The patches are generally worked in units, which are eventually joined to make the complete piece. Traditionally the units were square in shape or in the form of long narrow strips. But the method can obviously be adapted to individual requirements. With careful planning, it is possible to make units of unequal size and shape and individual paper

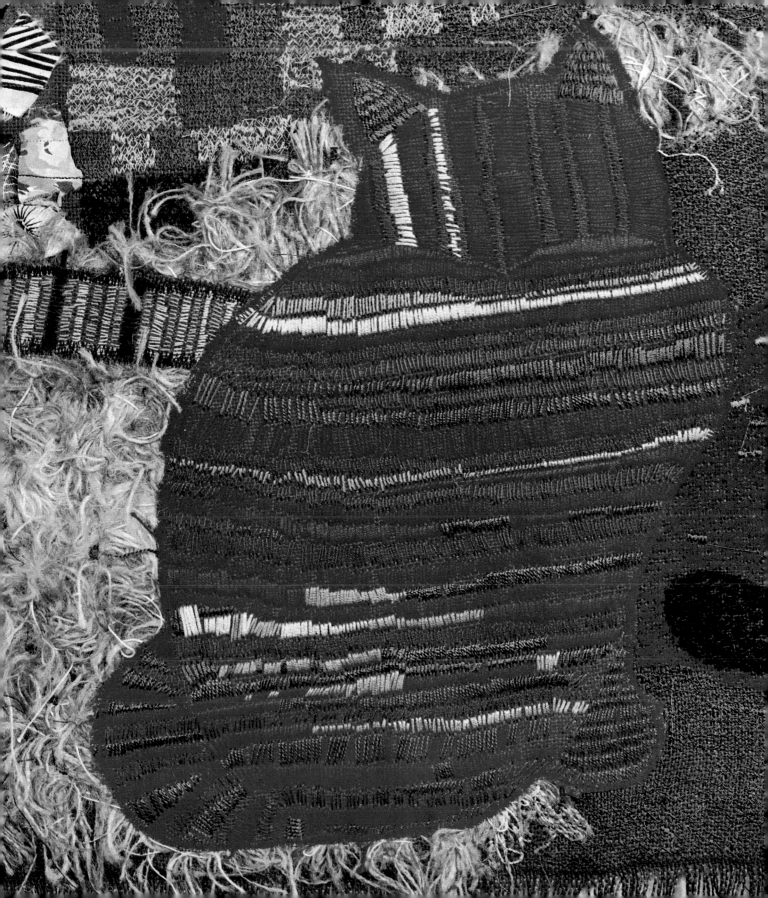

Detail of a panel of padded and stitched hessian by Danena Wrightson Hunt, 6 ft 6 in. × 10 ft (2 × 3 m). The embroiderer has the means to construct infinite varieties of texture. The design of this panel appears complex but the picture area is divided into relatively simple shapes. The focal point of the design is the contrast of an area of applied padded fabric with surrounding areas of rough texture: straight stitches in thick wool and strips and offcuts of fabric laced and applied to a background. Light-dark colour contrast is used to throw the padded area into greater relief.

patterns should be cut for these to serve as templates when cutting the foundation fabric. (The working method is illustrated by the method used for constructing one square of log cabin patchwork.)

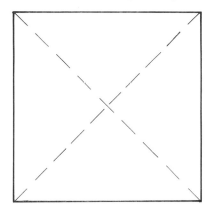 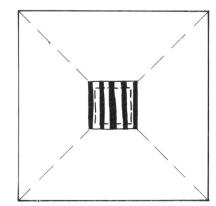

1 Cut a square of foundation fabric, calico (muslin) or cotton sheeting, to the required size with $\frac{1}{2}$ in. (13 mm) extra for seaming if several squares of log cabin patchwork are to be joined.

2 Stitch straight lines of tacking (basting) along the diagonals of the foundation fabric. Work the stitching from corner to corner so that they cross in the middle of the square.

3 Cut a small square of fabric to be used in the pattern and tack over the centre of the foundation fabric.

4 Cut four strips of fabric about 1 in. (25 mm) wide and sufficiently long to cover the edges of the centre square of fabric and just cover the diagonal line.

5 Pin a strip of fabric over the edge of one side of the square, and work a line of small running stitches about $\frac{1}{8}$ in. (3 mm) from the edge. When sewn, the strip is folded back over the stitching and pressed down.

6 Sew the second strip on the second side of the centre square, overlapping one end of the first strip.

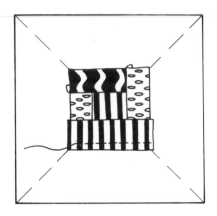 

7 Sew the third and fourth strips over the remaining sides of the square.

8 Cut four more strips about 1 in. (25 mm) wide and sufficiently long to cover the edge of the preceding row of strips and just cover the diagonal line.

9 Stitch in place covering the edges of the preceding row of strips.

10 Continue cutting and sewing strips of fabric in place until the whole foundation is covered. The last row of strips is folded down so that it meets the edge of the foundation fabric. The raw edges will be hidden when several units are joined. The edges of a single unit of log cabin patchwork can be turned under if it is to be applied to a further foundation.

CUTWORK

Cutwork is a form of embroidery in which entire parts of the fabric are cut away, resulting in patterns of fabric and holes.

In the past the technique developed into an elaborate form of embroidered decoration, the cut sections being worked in delicate lacy patterns of needle weaving in white thread on white fabric. Broderie anglaise or Madeira work is a coarse kind of cutwork that differs from earlier forms in that it does not include needlepoint fillings. Patterns are made up of small round or oval holes worked with overcast or button-hole stitch (pages 29 and 97). Richelieu embroidery, derived from early Italian cutwork, produces the opposite effect to broderie anglaise, the pattern being shown in solid white stitchery with the background cut away. The motifs are held together with worked bars. Ayrshire work combines cutwork with needlepoint fillings.

Only the basic methods of hand-stitched and machine-stitched cutwork, and of layered cutwork, are outlined here. The inventive embroiderer can use these to develop original patterns and designs. Try

54

Log cabin patchwork, 6 × 12 in. (150 × 305 mm). Traditionally the strips of log cabin patchwork are arranged around the four sides of a square but the method can be adapted to create individual designs. Some of the best effects in this type of patchwork are gained through the play and contrast of colour, pattern and tone, and it is ideal for showing the textural and reflective qualities of fabrics.

Shell and crazy patchwork combined in one design, 21½ × 14½ in. (546 × 370 mm). Rounded shapes and floral patterns in varying tones are contrasted with geometric shapes and patterns. The texture of corduroy is used, in the crazy patchwork, to complement the patterns of adjacent patches and give depth to the design. Both patchwork areas were worked as described in the text and then applied to a background of synthetic curtaining fabric.

placing several layers of cutwork one over the other, for example, the cut sections in a different position on each layer. Cutwork on plain fabric can be mounted on patterned fabric. Several fabrics can be 'patched' together before starting cutwork. By mounting cutwork it can then be padded or quilted.

Fabrics

In the past it was usual to use fine linen and cotton for cutwork. The fascinating range of fabrics available today enable the embroiderer to experiment with cutwork on many different types. Both natural and synthetic fabrics can be used, and should be chosen with the finished effect in mind. Delicate lacy effects are achieved by using an appropriately fine fabric. The edges of cut sections are likely to be more rough and uneven on open-weave fabrics, the best effects being achieved with the sewing machine. As a general rule, closely woven, soft pliable fabrics are best suited to the technique. Cutwork can be successfully worked on cotton lawn, calico and cotton organdie, linen crash and scrim, even-weave linen and synthetic fabrics, such as nylon, Terylene and rayon.

Threads

Threads should be chosen to suit the type of fabric: fine thread for lightweight and thicker thread for heavier fabrics. Even regular threads are ideal as they pass through most fabrics easily. Stranded cotton, coton-à-broder (embroidery cotton) and coton perlé (pearl cotton) should suit most fabrics. For machine-stitched cutwork, machine embroidery cotton Nos. 30 and 50 and mercerized sewing cotton No. 60 are suitable for most fabrics. The colour of threads can be chosen to match or to contrast with the colour of the fabric.

Hand-stitched cutwork

1 Mark out the shape to be cut away on the right side of the fabric, using fabric marker or tacking.
2 Work a line of small running stitches (page 88) around the outline of the previously marked shape.
3 Work buttonhole (page 97) or satin stitch (page 94) over the top of the running stitches.
4 When stitching is complete, cut away the fabric inside the shape. Small, sharp-pointed scissors are necessary for this purpose.

Machine-stitched cutwork

1 Mark the shape to be cut away on the right side of the fabric, using fabric marker or tacking.
2 Stretch the fabric on a ring frame.

3 Lower the feed of the machine or, in the case of old machines, place the cover plate in position and remove the presser foot. Thread the machine with embroidery or mercerized cotton and set both tensions slightly tighter than normal.

4 Machine around the outline of the previously marked area. Use a small straight stitch or fine zigzag. Two or three rows of stitching make a firm edge.

5 Cut away the fabric inside the outline shape. The space may be left as it is or filled with lacy patterns. The patterns are made by working interlinking lines of straight and zigzag stitch across the space. It is advisable to construct a framework of fine stitched cords (straight stitch) on which to build more elaborate patterns. Parts of lacy patterns could be emphasized with lines of close zigzag worked on top of the cords.

6 When the filling is complete, work close zigzag stitch around the cut edges. Cutaway shapes without lacy fillings may also be neatened in this way.

Layered cutwork (or reverse appliqué)

Two or more layers of fabric are stitched together and parts of each layer cut away to reveal the layer beneath. This effect is especially suited to intricate designs exploiting contrasts of different fabrics, the play of light on matt and shiny surfaces and textural effects in rough and smooth fabrics. The nature of the technique allows for great variety of design and both geometric patterns and shapes with intricate curves can be worked.

The number of layers that may be worked depends on the thickness of the fabric and the type of design. If the fabric is fine (lawn or viyella) as many as five or six layers could be combined. Generally only two or three layers of thick fabric (wool, tweeds, gaberdine) are advisable. If more are used, the whole unit can become stiff and unmanageable. Very small shapes (less than $\frac{3}{4}$ in. or 20 mm) are more successfully worked in fine fabrics, since it is difficult to sew through or cut away several layers of thick fabric.

Stitching has a dual function; it holds the fabric together and outlines the shapes and patterns. Straight or satin stitch (page 94) may be used, depending on the fabric and design. Straight stitch is relatively insignificant and is ideal for fluid designs. Satin stitch is more definite and bold and has the effect of emphasizing the edges of shapes.

1 Cut all layers of fabric to equal size.

2 Mark the pattern on the top layer of fabric, using fabric marker or tacking.

3 Place the layers one on top of the other and tack together.

4 Work a line of stitching around the edges of all shapes. Small back

Cutwork by Valerie Mosely, 9 × 12 in. (230 × 305 mm). Machine-stitched cutwork on two layers of fabric is used to make a lacy pattern of leaves with a three-dimensional effect; the fabric and holes playing equal parts in the design.

Layered cutwork by Valerie Mosely 9 × 12 in. (230 × 305 mm). Six layers of fabric have been cut to create a simple bold design which uses the textural effects of matt and shiny fabrics in different colours. The shapes were first outlined with a close zigzag machine stitch, then each layer cut separately.

stitch is suitable for hand work (several rows of stitching worked close together will ensure that the fabrics do not slip out of place). For machine-stitched cutwork, first work a line of straight stitch around the shapes (again several rows are usually necessary). Close zigzag could be worked over the straight stitching for a neat edge, and to hold frayable fabrics more firmly. Machine stitching can be worked with the presser foot on the machine as for normal machine stitching. Designs with intricate curved shapes are better worked with the presser foot removed (see page 115).

5 When stitching is completed remove the tacking. Cut away the areas of fabric on the top layer to reveal the fabric below. Where several layers have been worked cut away all the necessary portions on the top layer first, working down until the last layer is revealed. Raw edges must be protected with satin stitch if the article will be worn or handled.

For cutwork with turned and neatened edges, work through stages **1** to **3**, omit stage **4** and proceed as follows:

5 Cut away the areas of fabric but leave the tacking in place. Turn under the raw edges to make a hem and tack them down. Work tiny straight stitches at right angles and over the hemmed edges. The stitches should be $\frac{1}{8}$ to $\frac{1}{4}$ in. (3 to 6 mm) apart and taken through all the layers of fabric.

5 Fabric techniques II: padded and raised surfaces and three-dimensional forms

QUILTING

Quilting is a technique in which two layers of fabric are stitched together with a soft substance or wadding between them. The word quilt is derived from the Latin *culcita* meaning stuffed sack, mattress or cushion. During the last century, however, the word was used to describe almost any type of bedcover. This confusion may have arisen from the frequent practice of combining quilting techniques with other embroidery methods. Many so-called patchwork quilts and embroidered quilts in fact contain no quilting.

There are three main types or categories of quilting. The character of each is derived from the type of wadding used and the way it is stitched in place. Wadded quilting, often called English quilting, consists of two layers of fabric with an inner layer of wadding. All three layers are sewn together with stitched lines, giving an effect of depressed lines between softly raised areas. Wadded quilting can be made reversible if both outer layers of fabric are of similar quality. In the past the lines holding the three layers together and forming the pattern were of back stitch, chain and sometimes running stitch. Today these may still be used but a machine straight stitch can be substituted. In corded or Italian quilting two fabrics are sewn together with designs of close parallel lines of straight stitching making narrow channels. Quilting wool or cotton cord is threaded between the parallel lines. The overall effect is of raised lines on a flat ground. Stuffed or Trapunto quilting consists of two layers of fabric sewn together. Parts of the pattern made by the stitching are stuffed with wool or cotton to give raised areas on an otherwise flat background. The difference between corded and stuffed quilting is that the former is distinguished by raised lines whereas in stuffed quilting the padded areas can be of any shape. In shadow quilting a semi-transparent or transparent fabric is used for the top layer and a normal opaque fabric for the underneath layer. Coloured wool or cotton is stuffed or threaded between the layers.

Fabrics
The top layer of fabric should generally be soft and pliable enough to yield to the wadding, showing the pattern and technique to advantage. A list of such fabrics could include, cotton lawn and sateen, fine wool

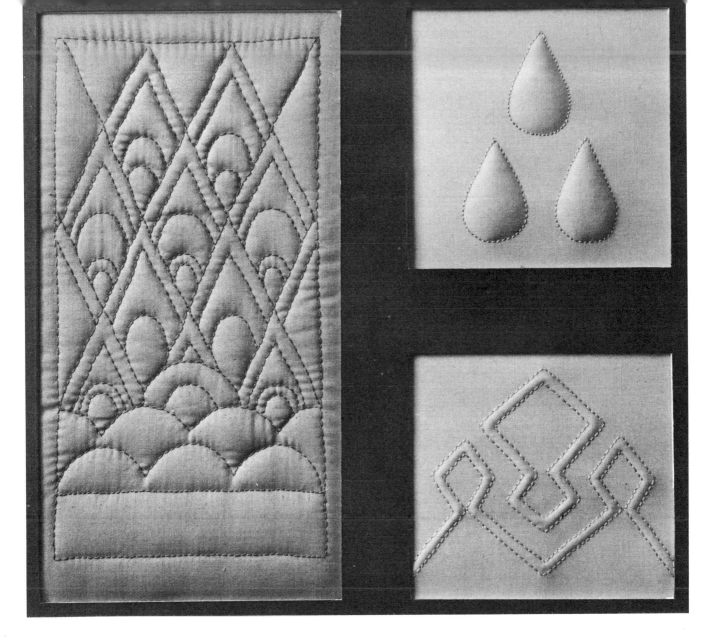

crêpe, lightweight silk, satin and some synthetic fabrics. Fabric for the bottom layer should be firm, to provide the necessary support for the wadding, stuffing or cord. If the fabric is too light these will show more on the wrong side of the work. Cotton sheeting, calico (light- and medium-weight) or fine linen are suitable. The middle layer can be of either natural or synthetic material. Cotton and wool domette are fairly thin, but several layers could be used to make a thicker padding. Terylene wadding is gaining in favour; it is easy to use and can be obtained in several thicknesses. Both cotton and wool quilting cord are available, but rug wool or knitting wool could be used.

(*left*) Wadded quilting: depressed lines between softly raised areas; (*above right*) stuffed quilting: raised areas on an otherwise flat background; (*below right*) corded quilting: raised lines on a flat background. The stitches form the design in quilting as well as holding the padding and fabric together; they can be worked in almost any arrangement of straight and curved lines, whether simple or elaborate. All three quilting techniques could be combined in one design.

Design for quilting

The final effect of quilting depends on the type of fabric used. Light and shade effects are more obvious on shiny fabrics, such as satin and silk. More subtle shadow effects are achieved with matt fabrics. And while light-toned and plain-coloured fabrics show quilting techniques to particular advantage, there is no reason why patterned and dark-toned fabrics should not be used.

Besides holding the fabrics and padding material together, the stitched lines also form the design or pattern. Virtually any design based on arrangements of straight and curved lines can be worked in quilting. The lines of stitching can either be worked to give simple outline shapes or grouped together to form more elaborate shapes and patterned fillings.

Each method can give varied results. Changes in the scale of shapes and patterns provide ample opportunity for developing original designs. All the quilting techniques can be combined in one design if so desired. Different parts of a design can be first worked with any of the quilting methods, and the quilted sections then brought together to complete the design, using an appliqué or patchwork method. Other types of embroidery can add interest to quilted fabric. Hand and machine stitches can be worked in areas between lines of corded quilting or around stuffed shapes and satin stitch gives pleasing effects when worked over corded quilting.

Wadded quilting (English quilting)

1 Mark the pattern on the right side of the top layer of fabric, using fabric marker or tacking.

2 Cut a piece of backing material (cotton, calico) and wadding (domette, Terylene or polyester) the same size as the top layer.

3 Place the three layers one on top of the other, the bottom layer of backing material first, then the wadding and finally the top layer of fabric.

4 The next stage can be worked in one of several ways. Small pieces of work can be put on to a ring frame. Larger pieces can be pinned to a rigid wooden frame or attached to a slate frame (see page 31). Do not use a frame when working machine-stitched quilting with the presser foot in position.

5 Stitch the three layers together, following the marked design on the top layer. Use back stitch (page 92) if the wadding is thin, stab stitch (page 28) if it is thick. The stitches should be small and even if the padded effect is to be successfully expressed. A machine straight stitch may be substituted if preferred. Normally the sewing thread is of the same colour as the top layer of fabric, since a different coloured thread could detract from the padded effect.

Stuffed quilting (Trapunto quilting)

1 Mark the shapes to be padded on the right side of the top layer of fabric, using fabric marker or tacking.

2 Place the backing fabric beneath the top layer and put them on to a frame. Small pieces of work can be made on a ring frame, larger pieces on a rigid frame (see page 27).

3 Tack the two layers of fabric together, avoiding where possible working over the outlines of the pattern.

4 Work lines of small running or back stitch to outline the shapes to be stuffed. A machine straight stitch may be substituted if preferred. Again the sewing thread should be the same colour as the fabric or a toning colour for patterned fabrics.

5 Turn the work over and make a small slit in the backing fabric only in the centre of the shape to be stuffed. Insert the stuffing (soft wool, kapok) through the slits. Take care not to overstuff the shape. The padded areas should stand up from the surface. but they should not be so full that they stretch the fabric and distort the design.

6 When the shape is stuffed draw the slit together using oversewing stitch (page 29) or herringbone (page 99).

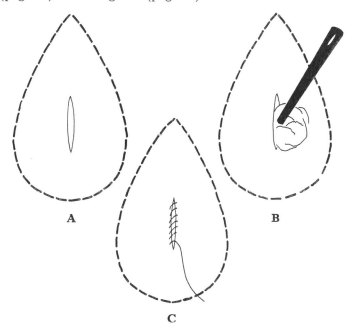

A   B

C

Stuffed quilting
A Outline the shape in stitching on the right side of the fabric. Turn the work to the wrong side and make a small slit in the backing fabric.
B Insert kapok.
C Oversew the slit

Corded quilting (Italian quilting)

1 Cut equal-sized pieces of backing and top fabric.

2 Mark the pattern on the right side of the top layer, using fabric marker or tacking. Remember that two parallel lines of stitching must be worked to make a line of corded quilting.

3 Place the backing fabric beneath the top layer and attach to a frame

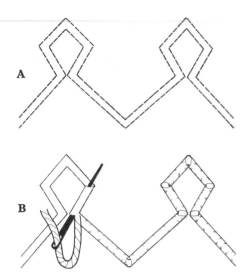

Corded quilting
A Outline the shape in stitching on the right side of the fabric.
B Insert the quilting wool at the back of the work along the channel formed by the stitched lines and between the two layers of fabric.

as for wadded quilting. No frame is necessary when working corded quilting on a machine.

4 Work back stitches along the marked pattern. Two lines of stitching are required to make a line of corded quilting. Machine straight stitch may be substituted. Sewing thread of the same colour as the top fabric is normally used.

5 Working on the back of the work, thread cord (wool, cotton or synthetic) through the two layers of fabric, between the parallel lines. Blunt large-eyed needles are useful for this purpose. The threading process is made easier if the thread is pulled through in stages: insert the needle through the backing fabric and bring up a short distance along the channel, pull the needle and cord through. Re-insert the needle where it last emerged and bring out a short distance along the channel. Continue threading in this way. To prevent the fabric from puckering, take care not to pull the cord too tightly.

Shadow quilting

This method is similar to corded and stuffed quilting, but the top layer of fabric is transparent, or semi-transparent, and the cord or stuffing is coloured. For the padding, cut shapes of strongly coloured fabric (felt is ideal for panels and hangings but it cannot be washed.) Tack or baste the padding in position on the background fabric. Lay a transparent fabric, such as organdie, on top of the shapes and tack in place. Work small running stitches round the edges of the shapes, stitching right through to the background. The colour of the padding needs to be bold if it is still to have some impact when viewed through the transparent fabric.

APPLIED PADDED FABRICS

Quilting techniques involve padding a continuous fabric surface and there is a limit to the amount of padding that can be used. Applied padded methods not only provide more scope for achieving raised effects, but also have special qualities of their own. With quilting the padded areas grow out of the fabric surface whereas applied padded shapes sit more on the surface of the embroidery and appear somewhat separate from it.

The embroiderer can include padded shapes and areas in an otherwise flat embroidery, at the same time introducing, if wished, a change in colour and fabric. Interesting effects arise from using padded shapes of different thicknesses in the same design. The addition of shapes initially worked with stitched appliqué or patchwork patterns and then padded widens the range of effects even further.

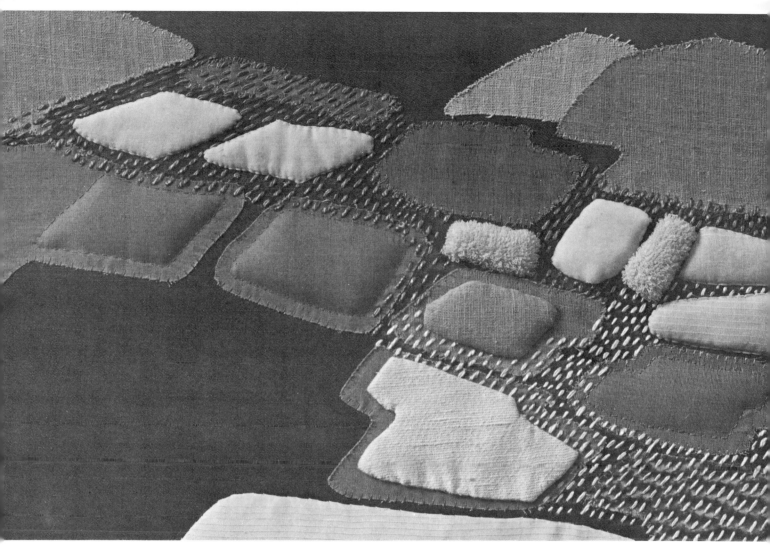

Wadding

1 Cut the shape the correct size out of wadding (Terylene, polyester or wool blanketing). Several layers may be used to make a thicker pad.

2 Pin the wadding to the wrong side of the fabric.

3 Trim the fabric to shape, using the wadding as a guide. A generous turning allowance is necessary, sufficient to turn down over the wadding without depressing the edge of the pad.

4 Fold the turning allowance down underneath the pad and tack in place. Any fullness on convex edges (circles, ovals, etc.), can be pleated and held in place with herringbone stitch (page 99). Over concave edges it may be necessary to snip at right angles into the turning allowance, and hold in place with herringbone stitch.

Applied padded shapes, 12 × 8½ in. (305 × 216 mm). A wide range of raised effects can be achieved by using shapes of different thicknesses and by combining them with appliqué and stitchery. Different fabrics introduce variations of colour and texture into the design and embroidery stitches can be worked on the padded areas or used, as above, to relate shapes to each other.

5 Sew the covered pad to the background fabric in a way chosen to suit the design. A smooth invisible join is made by slip stitching (page 29). A more decorative method is to work stab stitching (page 28) over the edge of the pad through the background material. Thin pads (one or two layers of padding) can be machine stitched to the background with straight or zigzag stitches.

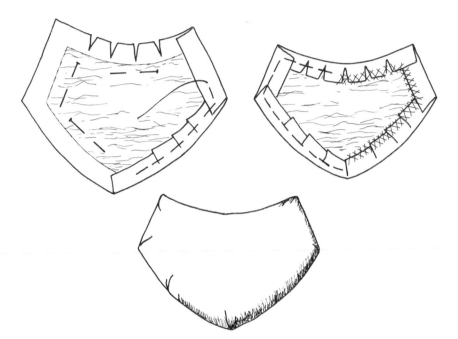

Wadding: the completed pad is cushion-like in appearance.

Felt pads

Shapes padded with felt produce a crisp and firm quality, while those padded with wadding are more soft and cushion-like in appearance. The number of layers of felt can be varied to give shallow relief effects or more pronounced raised effects. Some thick fabrics, such as corduroy, will not stretch smoothly and will have to be pleated round the edges of a thick pad. Therefore, if a smooth effect is required, avoid using thick fabrics. Most fabrics can be moulded over relatively thin pads, but flexible and stretch fabrics(knitted) respond readily to very thick padding. Thick padding is also successful with soft pliable fabric (crêpe and georgette).

1 Cut a number of similar shapes out of felt to form the layers of the pad. In pads consisting of two or more pieces of felt, the layers should gradually decrease in size. The largest forms the top of the pad and the smallest the base. When the layers are assembled they produce a rounded surface over which fabric is more easily and smoothly stretched.

2 Glue the layers of felt lightly together beginning with the largest layer and ensuring that all edges fit neatly to form the shape of the pad.

3 Place the pad on the fabric and use it as a guide to cut out the fabric shape. Cut the fabric with sufficient allowance to turn under the bottom of the pad.

4 Lay the fabric over the pad and pin and tack it in place on the underside.

5 Work herringbone stitch around the edge of the fabric to secure it to the felt.

6 Complete the process by sewing the covered pad to the background fabric. Slip stitch or stab stitch worked around the lower edge of the pad is normally quite adequate. Slip stitch is more easily worked if the background fabric is not stretched over a frame.

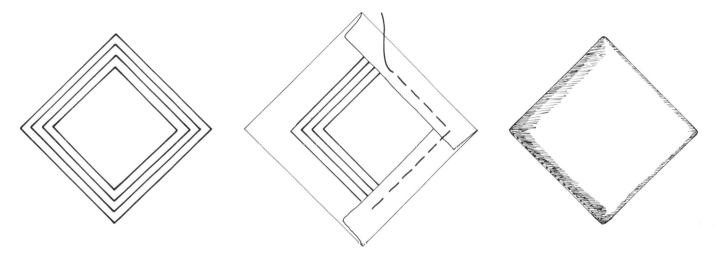

A slight modification to this process produces very different results. Layers of felt can be cut successively smaller, ½ in. (13 mm) or more, and placed one over the other to give a shallow stepped pyramid effect. Each layer of felt is covered with fabric and the layers are then stitched in position, starting with the largest. Each layer is stitched through the preceding layers. As many as six or seven layers could be used, depending upon the thickness of the covering fabric. The stitching process becomes rather more difficult when using thick fabrics and it is suggested that for first experiments two or three layers only should be used.

Felt pads: the completed pad has a crisp and firm quality. Use a thin fabric to obtain a smooth effect, especially over thick pads.

STITCHED PADDED AREAS

Padded shapes worked with stitching create interesting points of emphasis in a design. The shape is marked out on the fabric and stitched patterns worked within the outline. The stitched shape is then

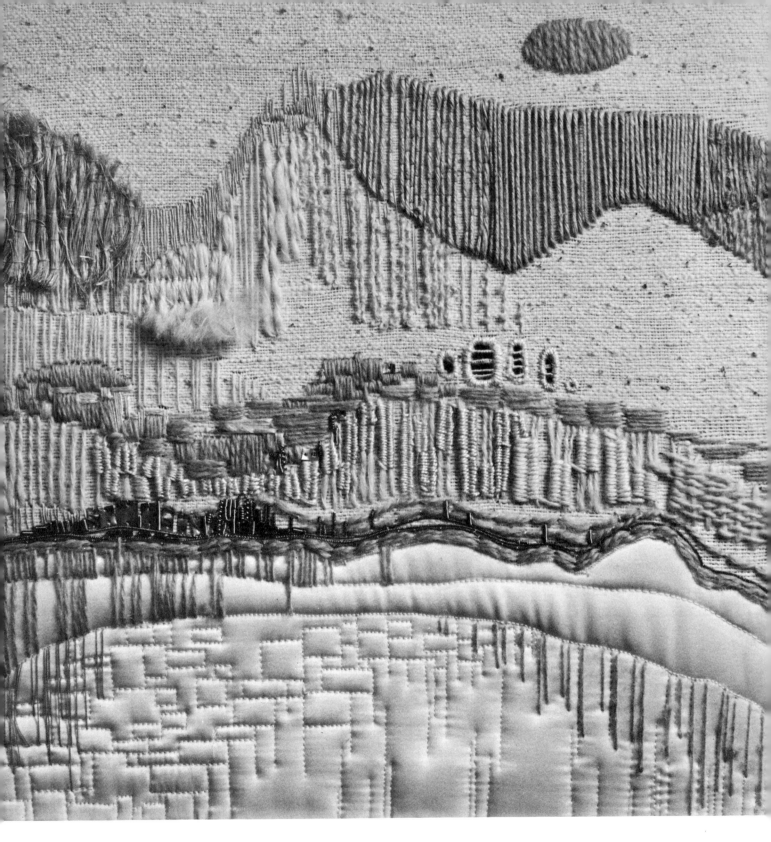

A stitched padded area in satin creates a shiny dimpled surface to contrast with the coarser textures of background and stitches. Machine stitch has been worked through both the fabric and wadding to produce this effect, and straight stitches in wool, worked over the padded area after it has been applied, help to integrate it into the design. Satin and straight stitches with couching in a variety of wool and string threads, together with beads and cutwork, form an interesting background. *Penarth* by Elizabeth Ashurst. 12 × 12 in. (305 × 305 mm).

cut out and padded by either of the methods mentioned above. Alternatively, stitched patterns and textures may be worked through fabric padded with soft wadding, creating a dimpled effect. The wadding is cut to shape and tacked to the wrong side of a larger piece of fabric. When the decorative stitching is complete, the fabric is cut to shape with a turning allowance. The allowance is turned over the wadding, tacked, and the padded shape slip stitched to the embroidery.

PADDED TRANSPARENT AND OPEN-WEAVE FABRICS

Apart from quilting techniques, transparent and open-weave fabrics (clear plastic, p.v.c. or sheet plastic, lace) can be padded in two other ways. Either pads of coloured felt, or felt or wadding covered with fabric, can be covered with a layer of transparent material. The process is the same as for other fabrics. N.B. If a pad is being covered with two layers of fabric (transparent and one other) it is easier to stitch each one separately.

Gentle restrained effects occur when both the colour and tone of the padding are closely related to the fabric. Patterns of lacy and open-weave fabrics can be emphasized by using a padding of contrasting colour or tone. As mentioned above, semi-transparent fabrics (organdie, cotton voile) will require a fairly strong coloured padding.

CARDWORK

Shallow relief can be produced by using different thicknesses of card as a support for fabrics. The fabric is drawn tightly down over the card and glued. The covered units are then attached to a firm base (card or wood). The attraction of this method is the smooth controlled surface of the firmly held fabric. The method is not suitable for any article to be washed or dry-cleaned. Shapes could be cut out with the grain of the fabric lying horizontally, vertically or diagonally to the background. Fabrics with a highly pronounced grain (corduroy) or fabrics with warp and weft of different colours (shot silk) are particularly suited to this treatment.

Closely woven light- and medium-weight fabrics, wild silk, surah, varieties of cotton, corduroy, velvet, have the necessary qualities for this method. The close weave allows sufficient flexibility for stretching over card, while at the same time providing a dense surface to which the glue can adhere. Card $\frac{1}{8}$ in. (3 mm) thick should be sufficiently strong to take the weight of most of the fabrics mentioned. Thinner card can be substituted for lighter-weight fabrics. Two layers of $\frac{1}{8}$ in. (3 mm) card could be cut to shape and glued together to make a thicker card which might be needed to support a heavier fabric such as corduroy or velvet. A firm base is necessary to support the covered units. Thick card is firm and strong enough to support small designs, but designs over 12 in. (300 mm) square are best mounted on thin hardboard. The technique is suitable for designs of not too large a scale, consisting of closely fitting shapes and patterns, similar to mosaic patchwork. More complex designs based on irregular shapes can be carried out, but great care must be taken to ensure that all the shapes fit well together. Variety may be created by combining this with other methods. Fabric could, for example, be decorated with stitched or appliqué patterns before being stretched over card.

1 Cut each shape out of card. Allow for the bulk of thicker fabrics by cutting the card unit slightly smaller than actual size.

2 Mark the shape on the wrong side of the fabric and cut out with a turning allowance of about $\frac{1}{2}$ to $\frac{3}{4}$ in. (13 to 20 mm) for gluing to the card.

3 Place the card shape on the wrong side of the fabric and spread a layer of fabric adhesive over the back of the card.

4 Press the turning allowance firmly down into position on the adhesive.

5 When the adhesive is dry, spread the back of each covered unit with a strong fabric adhesive and press into position on the base (card or wood).

N.B. The success of the completed design relies on a neat and accurate fit of all the covered pieces. To ensure a neat fit of irregular shapes, paper patterns could be used as a guide to cutting the card. A useful aid to accuracy is to mark the position of all the pieces on the base before gluing any of them in place.

THREE-DIMENSIONAL FORMS

Patchwork and quilting techniques used on a variety of small three-dimensional objects (pincushions, boxes and toys) have been popular for a long time. Padded and three-dimensional objects of a non-specific function are now being developed into a meaningful and legitimate medium for personal expression, to such an extent that 'soft sculptures' are now an accepted art form.

The simplest three-dimensional forms to make are geometric. Balls and spheres are also relatively simple. Irregular forms require more careful planning in the initial drafting stage, but with ingenuity it should be possible to work out the construction: failing this there are a number of books which will prove helpful (see Bibliography, page 145).

Three-dimensional forms simply made up in fabric can be interesting and attractive. Stitches, patchwork, appliqué, gathered, pleated and tucked fabric, beads, ribbons and cord, are effective methods and materials for developing patterns and designs on the surface of such forms.

There are certain important points to bear in mind before embarking on padded and three-dimensional works. First, it is usually advisable to make each section of the form individually, since it is easier to work stitches, appliqué and other embroidery techniques on flat fabric. Second, if a variety of different weights of fabric are to be used a foundation fabric will be necessary to provide a firm, even support, and to prevent fabrics from pulling out of shape when finally sewn together and padded. It also prevents lightweight fabrics from puckering when being worked with surface stitches. Third, it is wise to make paper patterns for each section of the form, to use as a guide for marking and cutting the fabric. Arrangements of shape and pattern on the surface of the form can also be marked on paper patterns. The fourth point to be considered is the making of an irregularly shaped form. It is useful in this case to construct the form in calico (muslin) or cotton sheeting before making up the final object. This procedure ensures that the correct shapes are achieved. If any modifications to the original pattern are required, they can be made on the calico shapes. The calico form can be unpicked and used as the pattern for cutting out the fabric. Alternatively, the modifications can be transferred to the paper patterns.

The choice of fabrics is a matter of personal preference. They may be selected for their textural, colour and pattern qualities. Almost any type of fabric could be used: corduroy, velvet, tweed, cotton lawn, wild silk, hessian (burlap). As mentioned previously, lightweight fabrics require a foundation material. Open-weave and stretch fabrics also require the support of a lining fabric, calico or a suitable colour of medium-weight cotton is adequate. Kapok, foam-rubber pads or chips are quite suitable for padding. Terylene and courtelle wadding is suitable for flattish shapes and forms. Small objects could be stuffed with kapok, cotton wool or a synthetic substitute. Old rags could be cut up and shredded and used for padding.

The working method can be broken down into stages to ensure that the final form is well designed and constructed successfully.

1 Plan the overall shape of the object, and decide which technique will be used.

2 Draw out the shape of each section of the form to size on drafting paper. The arrangement of shapes and patterns on the surface of the form may also be marked on the paper pattern.

3 Mark out the shape of each section on the fabric together with the shapes and pattern of the design, using paper patterns as guides. Where necessary tack or baste the foundation fabric to the top fabric.

4 Work stitches and any other techniques on to the marked shapes before cutting out the sections. (The procedure of cutting out the sections is left until stitching it is complete, thus preventing the fabric from stretching or fraying out of shape.)

5 There are two methods of joining the sections together. The first (A) is used for joining the pieces of three-dimensional forms with curved surfaces (spheres and balls) and for soft forms. The second (B) is used in the construction of straight-sided geometric forms.

A Seam all sections together (see page 43) using hand or machine stitching and leaving an opening through which the padding can be stuffed. The opening is later drawn together with oversewing or slip stitch.

B Stretch and lace each section of the form over card. For large three-dimensional objects, thin hardboard may be substituted. Join the sections on the right side of the object, with slip stitch or oversewing.

6 Fabric techniques III: folded and interrupted surfaces

In this chapter we shall consider the ways in which fabric can be folded, pleated, smocked, tucked and gathered. These methods have been known and practised for centuries on articles of clothing and furnishing. It is only recently that designers working in fabric and thread have started using them as a means of creating a variety of interesting surfaces. They may form only part of the embroidery, or the entire design can be developed from rippling surfaces of pleats, tucks and folds.

Apart from inherent differences produced by each method, pattern, textural and surface qualities derived from their use can be extremely varied. Many different effects can be created simply by altering the scale and spacing between individual pleats, tucks and folds. Different fabrics can be seamed together and treated similarly.

Both the method used and the nature of the fabric (matt, shiny, textured and pile) work together to produce interesting effects of light and shadow as well as of texture. The shadow effect is more pronounced when working with shiny and pile fabrics, although subtle effects can be gained from using other types of fabric.

PLEATS

The most common form of pleating consists of vertical folds held in place by a line of straight stitching worked across the top edge of the fabric. The pleats hang loosely from the stitched edge and are usually flattened or pressed down.

Pleated fabrics can be effective in embroidered designs. Areas can be covered with pleated fabrics attached at the top edge only, with the pleats hanging freely over the background. Alternatively, a crisper, more controlled effect can be achieved by stitching all the edges of the pleated sections to the background. Apart from applying separate sections of pleated fabric to an embroidery, the background itself could be pleated, to form part of the design. Patterned fabrics and those with warp and weft of different colours can be used to advantage. Changes in colour and pattern can be effected by making pleats vertically, horizontally and diagonally to the grain of the fabric. Different arrangements can be arrived at by grouping pleats with areas of flat fabric between

Sampler, 9 × 16 in. (230 × 406 mm). A rippling surface of pleats, tucks and frills shows to advantage on plain-coloured fabrics. Both the method and the nature of the fabric work together to produce interesting effects of light and shadow as well as texture. This sampler is worked in fine cotton lawn. Couched threads (machine stitched) and whipped running stitch give a slight textural contrast to the design of horizontal pleats and tucks.

them, by altering the width of individual pleats and by intermixing wide and narrow pleats.

1 Mark the size and shape to be covered with pleated fabric on the background material.

2 Cut a piece of fabric large enough to cover the marked area when pleated. Include a turning allowance of at least $\frac{1}{2}$ in. (13 mm) for pleated fabrics to be applied with turned edges. The method for gauging the amount of fabric for pleating is outlined below.

3 Fold the turning allowance under to the wrong side of the fabric and tack or baste.

4 Pleat the fabric and pin directly on to the previously marked area.

5 Stitch through the pleated fabric and the background material, working the stitches along the outer edges of the pleated fabric. Back stitch or machine straight stitch is normally adequate to hold the pleated fabric in position. Stab stitch (page 28) may be substituted for a less obvious stitched effect. Loose pleats are made by stitching the top edge of the pleated fabric to the background, leaving other edges to hang freely. The edges may be left raw or hemmed.

To gauge the amount of fabric required to pleat on to a specific area, one of two methods may be used.

A Take a piece of fabric larger than the previously marked area. Pleat and pin the fabric to the marked area. When a satisfactory arrangement has been found, use pins to mark on the pleated fabric the shape outlined on the background material. Remove the pleated fabric and cut away excess material. For hemmed or turned edges leave a turning allowance of $\frac{1}{2}$ in. (13 mm). This method is particularly useful for calculating the amount of fabric required to cover an area with irregularly pleated fabric.

B A more precise method of calculating the amount to be pleated into a specific area is illustrated here by the calculations for the amount needed to cover a rectangle 4 in. (100 mm) wide by 6 in. (150 mm) long with four vertical 1 in. (25 mm) pleats.

1 Mark out on the background fabric a rectangle 4×6 in. (100×150 mm).

2 The width of fabric needed for a pleat is double the size of the pleat: a 1 in. (25 mm) pleat requires 2 in. (50 mm) of fabric. Multiply the measurement of the amount of fabric taken up in the pleat, i.e., 2 in. (50 mm) by the number of pleats, i.e., four. The total in this case is 8 in. (200 mm).

3 Add 8 in. (200 mm) to the width of the shape, 4 in. (100 mm), to give a total of 12 in. (300 mm).

4 The fabric should therefore measure 12 in. (300 mm) wide by 6 in. (150 mm) long. Add $\frac{1}{2}$ in. (13 mm) turning allowance on all sides for hemmed or turned edges.

GATHERS

This is a simple process in which fabric is drawn into close, small folds by passing a thread (running or tacking stitch) through the material.

In embroidery gathered patches can be an effective way of throwing part of the pattern into relief. Ruffles and frills of gathered fabric and ribbon give an added play of light and shade. Several rows of frills can be placed close to each other to make a shape. Interesting effects can be achieved by gathering the whole of the background fabric, and developing the design in stitchery on the surface. Gathered effects can be altered by the size of the stitch used to draw the fabric together. The smaller the stitches, the finer the gathering. Different amounts of fabric can be gathered up into similar sized patches to produce a variety of effects.

The method works satisfactorily with most fabrics, although stiff varieties should be avoided. Soft materials such as voile, lawn, calico (muslin), velvet, wool and synthetic crêpe give very successful results when gathered.

Gathered patches in different textures are combined with applied padded shapes (page 66) and stitches in a design of squares which illustrates how effectively the play of light and shade can be used in an embroidery. Sampler, Goldsmiths' College, School of Art, London, 4½ × 4¾ in. (115 × 120 mm).

Small gathered patches

1 Mark out on the background fabric the size and shape of the area to be covered with gathered patches.

2 Cut a piece of fabric larger than the previously marked area. Include a turning allowance unless a raw edge is required.

3 For patches with turned edges, fold down the allowance to the wrong side of the fabric and crease.

4 Work running stitch around all edges of the patch about $\frac{1}{8}$ in. (3 mm) inside the edge.

5 Pull the running thread, gathering the patch until it is equal in size to the previously marked area.

6 Pin the patch to the previously marked area. Place patches with turned edges with the turnings facing the background fabric.

7 Stitch the patch to the background using small running stitches, working through the two layers of fabric and close to the edge of the patch.

8 Stab stitch through the two layers of fabric, working over the patch with enough stitches to prevent the fabric from ballooning out.

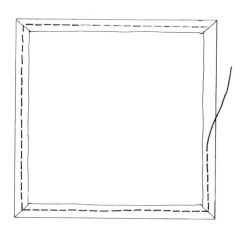 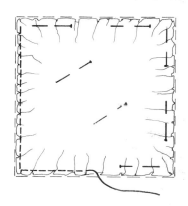 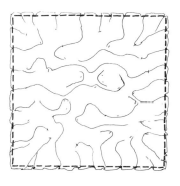

Large gathered patches

It is easier to use the following method for patches larger than 12 in. (300 mm) square.

1 Mark out on the background fabric the size and shape of the area to be covered with a gathered patch.

2 Cut a shape out of fabric, similar in shape but larger than the previously marked area. An extra 2 or 3 in. (50 or 75 mm) on the length of each side should produce a reasonable amount of gathering for covering areas of about 12 to 14 ins. (300 to 350 mm). For even larger areas, the amount of extra fabric on each side may be increased.

3 The edges of the fabric may be left raw. Alternatively, make a narrow turning by folding $\frac{1}{4}$ in. (6 mm) of fabric on all edges down to the wrong side of the patch. Tack or baste the turning.

4 Work several parallel lines of running stitch about 2 to 3 in. (50 to 75 mm) apart across the patch.

5 Pull the threads of running stitches until the patch is gathered up to the size of the marked area.

6 Pin the patch around the edges and at intervals over the marked area.

7 Work small running stitches on the two layers of fabric, stitching a short distance, $\frac{1}{4}$ in. (6 mm), inside the edge of the patch.

8 Work small stab stitches a short distance apart over the whole of the gathered surface, taking the stitches through both the patch and the background.

The running stitches holding the gathers may be retained as part of the effect, but they may be removed, if wished, as the stab stitching is sufficient to hold the gathers in place.

FRILLS

1 Cut a narrow strip of fabric, with an allowance for hemming if required. The strip may be cut straight with or across (on the bias) the grain of the fabric. Those cut straight with the grain are crisp. Frills cut on the cross fall gently and are fluted in appearance.

2 Hem both the long and short sides, or leave raw.

3 Start with a double back stitch and work a line of running stitch along one of the longer edges.

4 Push the fabric on the running thread until the required gathered effect is achieved.

5 Pin the frill to the background fabric.

6 Stitch with small running stitches or machine straight stitch close to the gathered edge.

This method can be adapted in the following way to make a double frill. At stage **3** work the running stitches down the centre of the strip. At stage **6** stitch along the running stitch line that holds the gathers.

TUCKS

Tucks are small pleats of fabric held in place with lines of stitching along the folds. The effect is ridges of fabric standing up from an otherwise flat surface.

Many different fabrics can be tucked successfully: soft ones such as crêpe, voile and lawn; crisp ones such as taffeta and denim, and thick ones such as velvet, wool and corduroy, give a variety of different qualities. Tucks can be stitched lengthwise on the straight grain, horizontally across or on the bias of fabric. In this way it is possible to alter the appearance of checked and striped fabric. Tucking effects show to particular advantage on plain-coloured fabrics, allowing for an obvious play of light and shade. Variations in texture can also be achieved.

1 Working on the right side of the fabric, fold and pin a narrow pleat in the material. With fine fabrics pleats $\frac{1}{8}$ to $\frac{1}{4}$ in. (3 to 6 mm) deep should be sufficient to make a noticeable tuck, whether horizontal, vertical or diagonal to the straight grain. Thicker fabrics may require larger tucks, $\frac{1}{4}$ to $\frac{1}{2}$ in. (6 to 13 mm) to make a significant difference.

2 Work a line of running stitch (or machine straight stitch) parallel to the folded edge following the pins.

Tucked fabric can be applied to a background in any one of the appliqué methods (see pages 40 to 44).

SMOCKING

In this method the fabric is gathered into regular folds held together with decorative stitching. Gathered surfaces produced by smocking can add interesting effects of surface pattern, texture, light and shade to an embroidery design. Smocked fabric could be applied to a background and used in conjunction with other kinds of embroidery. It works very well when combined with draped fabrics.

Fine and thick fabrics are equally suitable for smocking. Fine cotton lawn, cambric, linen, silk and cotton voile and organdie, cotton velvet and corduroy, fine and thick wools of various kinds, linen scrim, and many synthetic fabrics, produce a wide range of effects.

Threads should be smooth enough to pass through the fabric easily. Stranded cotton, coton-à-broder (embroidery), coton perlé (pearl), silk thread and many even-spun knitting and crochet yarns could be used. The type of thread will depend upon the nature of the fabric. Shiny threads, stranded cotton, coton-à-broder, perlé and silk thread are best for working on fine, closely woven fabrics and for velvet and corduroy. Wool threads and cotton, silk, and linen thread are equally suitable for wool and linen fabrics. Open-weave fabrics can be stitched with almost any type of thread.

1 With a fabric marker mark on the wrong side of the fabric the positions for the gathering stitches; a small dot is adequate. Use pins to mark open-weave fabrics. A ruler is useful for marking the positions. The spaces between the gathers are usually equal but may be varied. The distance between each row of dots may also be equal or

Smocking
A The positions for gathering marked with small dots.
B The threads are pulled and tied to form folds in the fabric.
C Stem stitch is worked across the gathered fabric.
D Rows of stitches can be worked right across the fabric or over only a few gathers.

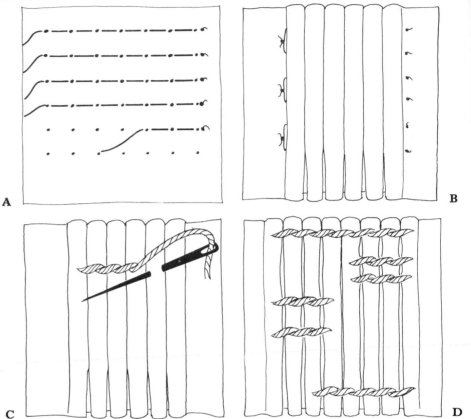

varied. Equal spacing will, when stitched, make regular patterns. Varied spacing will give uneven effects. Regular transfer patterns of dots can be bought.

2 Using a thread of sufficient length to complete each row, work a line of tacking stitches along the rows of dots. Pick up a few threads of fabric where the dots are marked. On completion of each line leave the end of the thread loose.

3 When the required number of rows has been stitched, hold the loose ends of thread, and ease the fabric along until the required width of gathering is obtained.

4 Insert pins at the end of each row of tacking close to the edge of the last fold of fabric and wind the loose threads around them. The folds can then be adjusted until a satisfactory arrangement of gathers is achieved. Then remove the pins two at a time and tie the pairs of threads together. The right side of the fabric now consists of a series of folds or 'tubes'.

5 With the right side of the work facing upwards, work a line of stem stitch right across the gathered fabric. Begin working with a knot at the end of the thread, bring the needle up through the first fold of fabric and pick up a small portion of each successive fold. The needle can be inserted into the fold either in a slanting direction or horizontal to the fold. The direction of the needle will influence the final effect of the stitching.

Rows of stitching can be worked across the complete surface or areas of gathers can be worked with groups of stitched lines. Sufficient groups must be worked to hold the gathered fabric together when tacking threads are removed. Lines of stem stitch worked in different arrangements should provide sufficient scope for creating varied patterns.

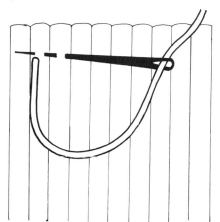
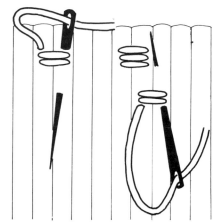
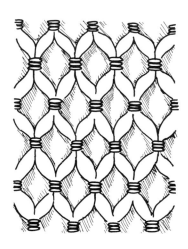

Honeycomb pattern

A kind of honeycomb, with cellular cavities, can be made in the following way.

1 Working from left to right on the gathered fabric bring the needle up through the first fold and pick up a small piece of fabric from the second and first fold. The needle is inserted just horizontal to the folds. Draw the thread through.

2 Work another stitch above and close to the first stitch. Draw up the stitches firmly to hold the folds together.

3 Insert the needle just above the last stitch on the second fold and slip it downwards along the back of the fold. Bring out a short distance from the first three stitches.

4 Work two stitches on the second and third folds and insert the needle, slipping it upwards on the third fold to emerge a short distance above.

5 Work stitches as before over the third and fourth folds. The work continues in this way working groups of stitches first above and then below an imaginary horizontal line across the work. The gathering thread (tacking) could be used as a guide line.

Honeycomb pattern. To make a regular pattern work the groups of stitches across the folds in line with each other and regularly spaced.

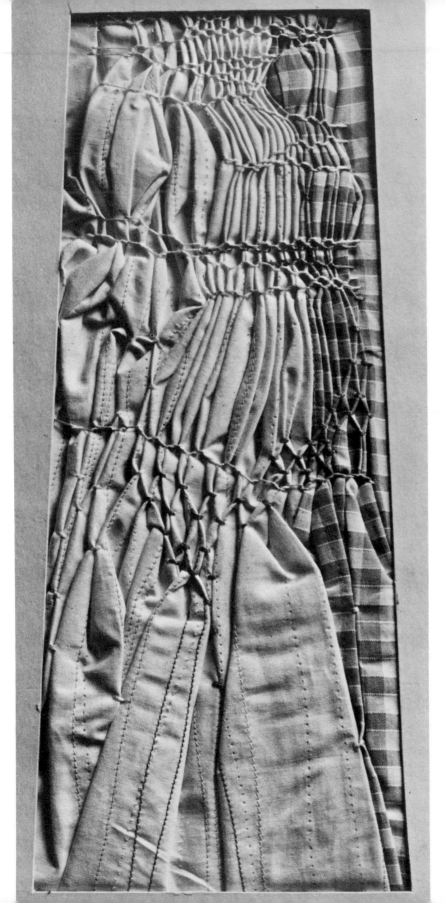

The technique of smocking is freely adapted to a design in which areas of loose vertical ridges are contrasted with areas of cell-like cavities. The effect of light and shade created by the technique is enriched by the use of patterned and plain cotton fabric. The stitching, although functional in that it holds the folds of fabric together, also gives additional pattern and texture to the design. Smocking by Julia Bullmore, 5 × 12 in. (130 × 305 mm).

To make a regular pattern work the groups of stitches across the folds, in line with each other and regularly spaced.

Irregular patterns are made by varying the length of the stitch worked under the fold. Patterns can also be varied by leaving some of the folds unstitched. Again, care must be taken to work sufficient stitching to hold the gathered fabric together when the tacking stitches are removed.

DRAWN AND PULLED THREAD WORK

Drawn thread is a method in which some of the warp and weft threads of the fabric are removed. In its simplest form, threads are removed in one direction only, either warp or weft. The remaining threads are worked with stitches to produce lacy open-work patterns. More elaborate forms of drawn thread are produced when both warp and weft threads are removed from areas of the fabric: this is a form of cutwork (see page 54).

In pulled thread the warp and weft threads are not removed but pulled together with firm and tightly worked stitches to produce spaces (or holes) between the threads of the fabric.

Drawing the threads is easier if a fairly loosely woven fabric is used. In the past, delicate lacy patterns were worked in this method on fine, evenly woven linen. Linen is still suitable but other fabrics may also be used: linen scrim, sacking, loosely woven tweeds and woollens. Many modern curtaining fabrics are loosely woven and are valuable additions to the range of fabrics that may be used for drawn and pulled work. Varieties of fabrics constructed of loosely linked yarns are also suitable.

Most usual embroidery threads, cotton, silk and linen, may be used for working these kinds of embroidery. Choose a thread which can be pulled tightly through the fabric without breaking. Knitting and crochet yarns, natural and synthetic raffia and even thread removed from the fabric add to the range which may be used. Machine embroidery cotton and mercerized cotton are used for machine drawn thread work.

Drawn thread work
It is best to work the first piece of drawn thread work in a simple shape such as a rectangle. Once you have become familiar with the working process other shapes can be attempted.
1 Mark out on the fabric the area to be worked.
2 Cut either the warp or weft threads one at a time in the centre of the marked area. Ease each cut thread out of the fabric.
3 The cut threads can either be woven into the edges of the shape or turned under to the wrong side of the fabric and stitched in place.

(*above*) Drawn thread work by Jane Iles, 6 × 6 in. (150 × 150 mm). An effective design achieved by removing warp and weft threads and binding groups of weft threads together with buttonhole stitch. Use simple shapes and loosely woven fabrics for early attempts, but more intricate designs can be produced by contrasting areas of drawn thread work with areas in which the fabric is left intact.

(*right*) Pulled thread work by Jane Iles, 4½ × 7½ in. (115 × 190 mm), in which back, running and overcast stitches are used, together with various pulled thread stitches (see *Dictionary of Embroidery Stitches* page 145). Patterned effects are produced by varying the number of threads pulled together and by working the stitches in different directions.

4 The remaining threads can be worked in a variety of ways. Groups of threads can be bound together with oversewing and buttonhole stitch (page 97). Raised chain bands (page 96) and portuguese border stitch (page 100) can be worked using the threads of fabric in place of laid straight stitches. Groups of threads can be bound and sewn in irregular arrangements or worked into formal patterns.

Pulled thread work

There are over fifty pulled thread stitches, many of which are described in various dictionaries of stitches (see Bibliography, page 145). It is suggested that these be referred to for working more formal and traditional types of pulled thread work. The following is intended to outline the basic process which, with the range of fabrics and threads available today, can be adapted to achieve a variety of different effects.

Stitches should be worked over several threads of fabric and must be pulled tightly, to achieve the open-work effects characteristic of the method. The threads of fabric are pulled firmly together with tightly worked stitches either horizontally or diagonally, and sometimes vertically. Buttonhole and satin stitch (page 94) are the simplest stitches that can be worked effectively. Several parallel rows of stitches may be worked to produce larger spaces between the threads of fabric. The number of threads pulled together can be varied. Larger spaces can be achieved by using a fabric with a more open weave.

7 Hand stitchery

Stitchery is the one technique that is easily combined with and enriches all the other techniques. The first steps towards discovering the range of effects that can be achieved with stitches can be made through working experimental pieces, the modern equivalent of the 'sampler'. But while samplers were a means of learning and arranging stitches in an accepted pattern, it is hoped that the embroiderer today will feel free to adapt and modify stitches in a personal and individual manner.

The unique qualities of stitches are derived from the texture and play of light on threads, the nature and form of individual stitches, and the interaction between fabric, thread and stitch. The texture of the fabric is important: a stitch appears to lie on the surface of smooth fabric, but integrates with or sinks into textured fabric. Smooth, shiny threads worked on to matt or rough fabrics, or matt threads worked on shiny fabrics produce striking contrasts. Stitches worked in thread similar to the fabric yarn are more likely to produce harmonious results. Integrated textures can be created by combining richly textured fabric and slubbed or knobbly threads.

The amount of stitchery worked in an embroidery is a matter of personal preference. In some designs, unworked areas of fabric contrast with detailed areas of pattern and texture in stitchery, in others the effect made depends entirely on stitches.

Bullion knots with straight stitches and detached chain stitches. The effect of this design is created entirely from the physical properties of the stitches used in it: the contrast in their form and texture; the play of light on thread; and the interaction of the fabric with thread and stitches. Some of the most pleasing results are obtained by arranging stitches in the simplest manner. Sampler by Linda Flower 5 × 7 in. (130 × 180 mm).

LINE AND STRAIGHT STITCHES

Running stitch

This is a line stitch and the simplest of embroidery stitches. The thread is passed over and under threads of fabric, producing on the right side of the fabric a line of straight stitches with spaces between them. Bring the needle and thread up from the back of the fabric to the right side. Insert the needle a short distance from where it first emerged, down to the back of the fabric. Bring the needle up again to the right side and a short distance from where it was last inserted. Pull the thread through. The movement of the needle and thread is continued in this way until a line of stitches is worked.

The length of stitches and the distance between them may be varied. Experiment by working stitches in curved, straight and crossed lines.

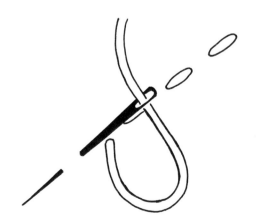

Porcelain by Margaret Hall, 9 × 7 in. (230 × 180 mm). Closely laid couched threads are used to make decorative fluid patterns against unworked areas of fabric. The flowing lines are interrupted by areas of seeding and intricate shapes of french knot and satin stitch. Compare the marvellous detail of pattern and texture in this embroidery with the simplicity of that on page 70.

Threaded running stitch

First a line of running stitches is worked. On the right side of the work a needle and thread is passed under the line of running stitches, threading them alternately from the left- and right-hand sides. At this stage the needle and thread do not pass through the fabric.

The same or different threads can be used for the threading. Try combining matt and shiny threads. A long running stitch can be threaded with narrow ribbon, cord or strips of fabric. Two or more rows of running stitch can be threaded together.

A Threaded running stitch
B Whipped running stitch
Linear patterns can be made from lines of running stitch; their width varied by the use of fine or thicker threads, different sizes of stitch, or by working several lines parallel to each other.

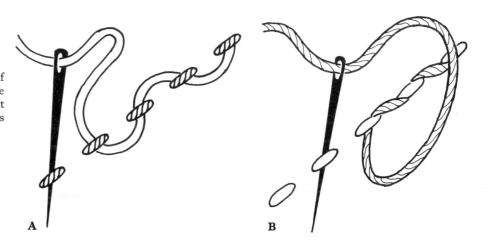

Whipped running stitch

A foundation of running stitch is worked. A thread is then passed over and under the line of running stitch. Working from the top of the line pass the needle from the left-hand side downwards and under the first running stitch. Repeat the movement on the second and subsequent stitches until the line is covered with the second thread. Different threads may be used for whipping. Try whipping with different coloured threads twisted together.

Back stitch

This stitch is worked from right to left on the fabric. The needle is brought out a short distance along from the beginning of the line to be stitched. It is inserted back at the beginning of the line (in effect taking a 'step' backwards) and brought up an equal distance beyond where it first emerged. The needle and thread are pulled through ready for the next stitch. The needle is then inserted at the point where it first came through, thus making a stitch on the back of the work twice as long as on the front. Small back stitches are often used in plain sewing, for appliqué and for seaming fabrics together.

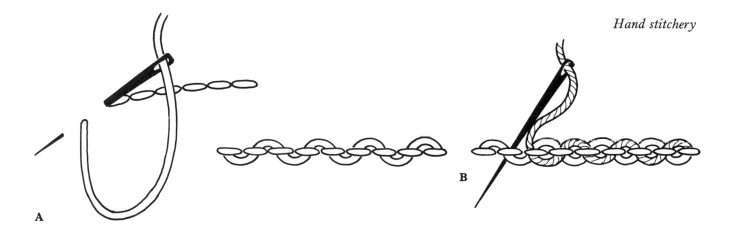

Threaded back stitch

Back stitch is threaded in the same way as threaded running stitch.

Back stitch and threaded back stitch may be worked to outline a shape. Several lines of stitches using different threads will produce interesting textural effects.

A Back stitch
B Threaded back stitch. A useful stitch for obtaining raised effects with threads that do not pass easily through a closely woven fabric.

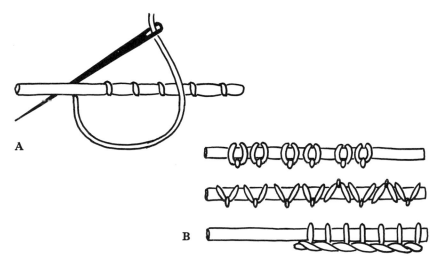

A Couching
B Couching with chain, fly and buttonhole stitches.

Couching

This is a method in which threads are laid on the surface of the fabric and held in position with stitches worked over them. Bring a thread out at the right-hand end of the line to be covered and hold flat on the fabric. Bring a second thread out close to the end of the first thread and to one side of it. Insert the needle on the other side of the laid thread and bring the needle out farther along the line and on the other side. This movement produces a small vertical stitch over the laid thread. Continue stitching in this manner until the thread is secured to the fabric. To finish off neatly take both threads through to the back of the fabric. Thick threads can be oversewn with the same or a thinner

93

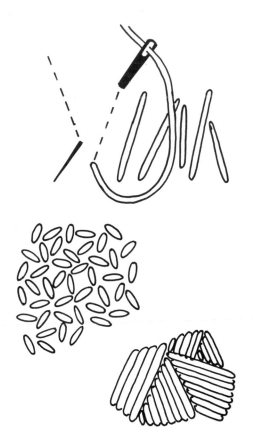

thread. Different effects can be achieved by working other stitches, chain, fly or buttonhole stitch (page 97), for example, over the laid thread. Experiment by working couched threads close together to make a dense area of thread. Try couching a matt thread with a shiny thread. Cord, narrow ribbon and strips of fabric can be couched.

Straight stitch

Straight stitch consists of single isolated stitches of any length. The needle is simply brought up through the fabric and inserted some distance from where it first emerged. The stitches may be worked in different lengths and in any direction. Interesting effects can be achieved by working straight stitches over each other and by combining different threads of various colours.

Seeding

Seeding consists of small straight stitches of even length worked at different angles. To achieve the best results they should be distributed irregularly over the surface with no attempt to arrange them into a pattern. An area of seeding can be worked in different coloured threads. The stitches can be massed densely or spaced wide apart.

Satin stitch

This stitch consists of straight stitches worked parallel to each other. The stitches should lie close and even. They may be any length and worked in any direction. Very long satin stitch may sag unless the work is stretched on a frame.

Satin stitch can be worked to fill almost any shape. Try working a second row of stitching on top of the first, in the opposite direction.

KNOTTED, LOOPED AND TWISTED STITCHES

Chain stitch

This is a fairly simple stitch that may be worked single (detached chain stitch) or in a continuous line.

To work a line of chain stitch bring the thread up through the fabric and hold down with the left thumb. Insert the needle where it last emerged and bring out a short distance from where it entered. Pull the thread through, keeping the loop under the needle. The next stitch is then worked by inserting the needle where it last emerged and following the same procedure.

Try working straight and curved lines of chain stitch. Lines of chain stitch worked close together produce a surface rather like knitted fabric.

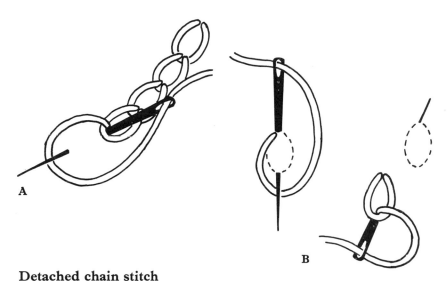

A Chain stitch
B Detached chain stitch
C Back-stitched chain stitch
D Whipped chain stitch

Detached chain stitch

The stitch is worked in the same way as chain stitch, but each stitch is fastened with a small stitch at the foot of the loop. Try working stitches at different angles to each other or all in the same direction. Group them together to make shapes.

Back-stitched chain stitch

A line of back stitch can be worked down the centre of a row of chain stitch. A contrasting coloured thread will show most effectively. Like the running stitches, this stitch can be worked in curved or straight lines, used to outline a shape or massed together to make a texture.

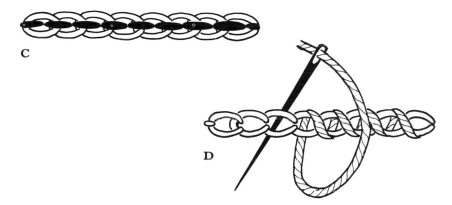

Whipped chain stitch

A row of chain stitch can be whipped or threaded with a matching or contrasting thread. The thread is passed under each chain stitch in a similar way as for whipped and threaded running stitch.

Twisted chain stitch

It is easier to work this stitch downwards on the fabric, with the needle pointing towards you. It may be worked in a continuous line or as a single stitch.

To work a line of twisted chain bring the thread up through the fabric at the top end of the line to be covered. Hold the thread down on the fabric with the left thumb. Insert the needle just below where the thread emerged and to the left of it. Bring the needle out in a slanting direction a short distance from where it was inserted. Pull the thread through with the working thread looped beneath it. The next stitch is made as before, inserting the needle close to the last stitch.

Experiment by working a line of twisted chain, alternating small and large stitches. To alter the size of the stitch, take up more or less fabric when the needle passes to the left of the thread. Lines of this stitch can be grouped together to make a textured area.

Detached twisted chain stitch

This is worked as for twisted chain stitch but each loop is secured at the foot with a small straight stitch.

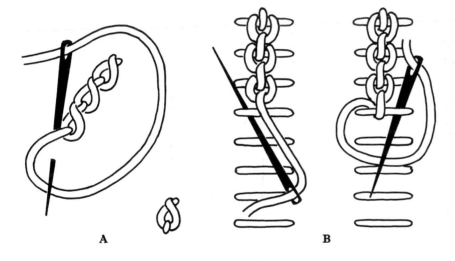

A Twisted chain stitch and detached twisted chain stitch
B Raised chain band. This stitch can be used successfully in drawn thread work (pages 85–7), the threads of fabric replacing the foundation of laid straight stitches.

Raised chain band

This stitch is worked on a foundation of short straight stitches laid parallel and a short distance apart. Bring the thread out just above the centre of the first straight stitch. Pass the needle over the first thread and then upwards beneath it so that the needle emerges at the top but to the left. The thread is then held downwards and the needle passed from the top right-hand side downwards underneath the first laid thread. The thread is drawn through with the loop underneath the needle. The next stitch is worked on to the second laid thread in the same manner. Stitching continues until all laid threads are covered. If the foundation stitches are sufficiently wide, several rows of stitching can be worked on them, producing a solid band. Interesting effects can be achieved by working the foundation of straight stitches with varying distances between them.

Buttonhole stitch

This stitch is worked from left to right across the fabric. Bring the needle up through the fabric and insert a short distance above and to the right of where the thread first emerged. Take a straight stitch down behind the fabric and bring the needle through level with the point where the thread first emerged. Keep the thread beneath the needle point and pull through. The next stitch is worked in the same way. The stitch may be worked back from right to left when convenient.

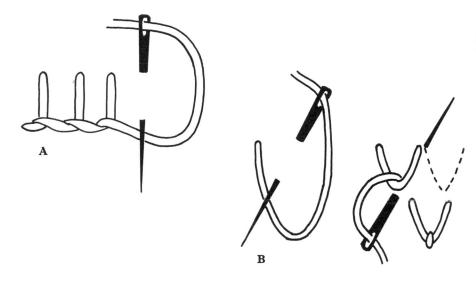

A Buttonhole stitch
B Fly stitch

Fly stitch

Bring the thread up through the fabric and hold down with the left thumb. Insert the needle to the right and level with the point where the thread first emerged. Take a small slanting stitch towards the centre of the two points and pull through with the thread beneath the needle. Complete the stitch by taking the thread to the back over and just below the loop. The length of the holding stitch at the bottom of the loop can be varied.

Fly stitch can be worked in any direction on the fabric and arranged irregularly or grouped into patterns. Stitches of different sizes can be worked closely together or farther apart to make an area of texture. The stitches can be overlapped, worked in the same direction or in different directions.

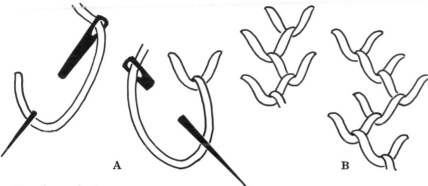

A Feather stitch
B Double feather stitch
A more compact effect is obtained by pointing the needle downwards through the fabric instead of slanting the stitches.

Feather stitch

Bring the thread through to the right side of the fabric and insert the needle to the right and level with where it last emerged. Take a small slanting stitch towards the centre of the two points and pull through with the thread running beneath the needle. Insert the needle a short distance to the left of where it last emerged and take a small slanting stitch towards the centre. Pull the thread through as before. The next stitch is worked to the right. Stitching continues in this way working alternately from left to right.

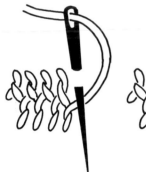
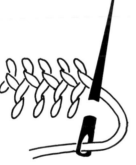
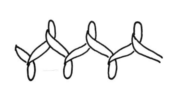

Variations of cretan stitch. Cretan stitches can be worked very close together as an even filling stitch, or as an open feathery line.

Cretan stitch

This stitch is usually worked from left to right across the fabric; if wished, it may be worked from right to left. Bring the needle up through the fabric and insert above and slightly to the right of this point. Bring the needle out a short distance above the point where the thread first emerged. Pull through with the thread underneath the needle. The needle is then inserted a short distance to the right and below the first stitch. Take a small stitch upwards with the thread below the needle and pull through. Stitching continues in this way with the stitches being first worked downwards and then upwards.

Variations of cretan stitch can be made by shortening or lengthening the amount of fabric taken up by the needle, and by altering the distance between stitches. Cretan stitch gives interesting effects when several lines are worked one over the other. Try using different threads.

98

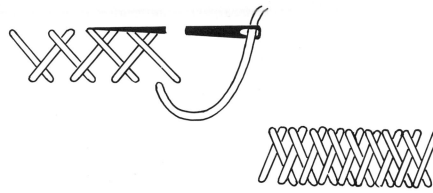

Herringbone stitch

This stitch is worked from left to right, and along an imaginary double line. Bring the thread out on the bottom line. Insert the needle to the right and on the upper line and bring out a short distance to the left and level with the point of insertion. Pull through. Work the next stage on the lower line. Insert the needle to the right of the first stitch and bring out a short distance to the left and pull through. The stitch is then repeated working alternately on the top and bottom lines. Like the cretan stitch, herringbone can be worked in lines, one over the other.

French knot

The thread is brought through at a point where the knot is required. The thread is held with the left thumb and first finger. The needle is twisted round the thread once, turned round and the point inserted close to the place at which the thread first emerged. French knots can be massed together to make a knobbly texture.

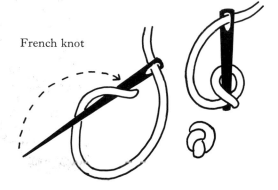

French knot

Bullion knot

Bring the thread up through the fabric and make a straight stitch the required length of the bullion knot. Do not pull the needle through but leave it lying on the fabric. Twist the thread round the needle as many times as is required to fill the space of the straight stitch. Hold the coil with the left thumb and pull the needle through carefully. Turn the needle back to the point of insertion, taking it through in the same place. Pull the thread through until the coil lies flat. Experiment by using knots of thin and thick thread in one area to create different textures.

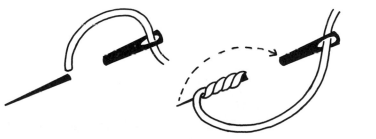

Bullion knot

99

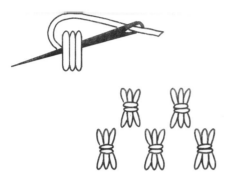

Enchanted Garden by Frieda F. Hidma, 6 × 9 in. (150 × 230 mm). Machine embroidery need not be a limiting medium; a great variety of textural qualities can be expressed with only the straight and zigzag stitches most sewing machines produce. Create streaked effects and crosshatching with lines of straight stitches, and smooth evenly filled areas with zigzag stitches closely worked to resemble satin stitch. Scribbled and grained effects can be made by couching thicker threads in loops and knots. Compare the different effects achieved in this work with the embroideries on pages 114–18.

Sheaf filling stitch

This stitch consists of three vertical satin stitches bound together with two overcast stitches (page 29). First work three satin stitches and bring the needle up beneath them on the left side. Make two overcast stitches around them. The needle does not enter the fabric until the second binding stitch has been made; then take it down through the fabric. Sheaf filling stitch can be worked into an organized pattern, grouped at random or mixed with other knotted stitches.

Spanish knotted feather stitch

Bring the thread through and hold down to the left. Insert the needle above the thread and make a small slanting stitch to the left. Pull the thread through with the loop under the needle. Insert the needle above the first stitch and make a small slanting stitch to the right. Pull the thread through. Continue in this way working downwards to the left and to the right, each time inserting the needle just above the last stitch.

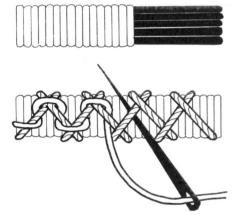

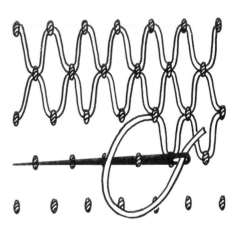

Lattice band raised

First lay a foundation of long straight stitches, parallel and close together. (To achieve a rounded surface a second layer of straight stitches can be placed over the centre of the first band.) Then cover the foundation with satin stitch and work a row of herringbone over it. The needle enters the fabric just above and below the padding. Complete the stitch by lacing a thread under and over the herringbone. This stitch is effective with many of the line stitches.

Portuguese border stitch

Work a band of parallel straight stitches about $\frac{1}{6}$–$\frac{1}{4}$ in. (4–6 mm) apart. Work four satin stitches over the lower two bars without the needle entering the fabric. Insert the needle through the fabric just above the second bar and emerge just below it. Work two satin stitches over the second and third bars and a small stitch over the third bar. Continue stitching two bars at a time working from the outside towards the centre. On the left side work from the centre outwards.

Cloud filling stitch

Make a foundation of small vertical straight stitches placed in rows at regular intervals as shown in the diagram. Then lace a thread through the foundation stitches by slipping the needle first under an upper stitch and then under a lower one. Different effects can be achieved by altering the spacing of the vertical stitches, placing them closer or farther apart. Contrasting threads can be used for the foundation stitches and lacing thread.

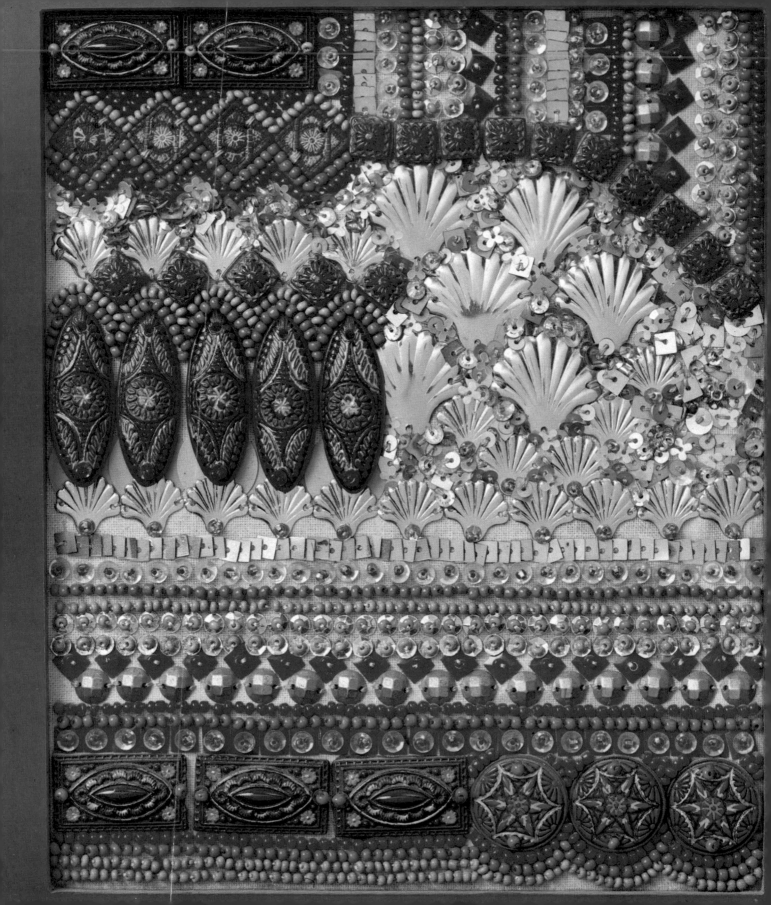

An ordered profusion of beads and sequins makes a rich design in *Anatolia* by Dorothy Darch, 5 × 6½ in. (130 × 165 mm). Their shapes, colours and textures are used and contrasted to achieve the most effective pattern. Anything that can be held in position with threads can be used with embroidery to create contrasts of texture and to add emphasis to a design.

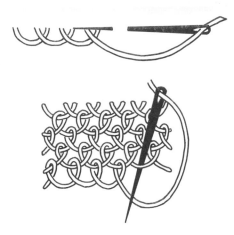

Buttonhole filling stitch

Begin this stitch by working a line of loose detached loops, overlapping as shown in the diagram. Then work a line of buttonhole stitch on to the loops, the needle only entering the fabric at either end of the row of stitches. This creates a second row of loops. Continue working buttonhole from left to right and right to left across the area to be filled. The effect can be varied by altering the size of the stitches.

Couched filling stitch

A simple but decorative stitch consisting of long vertical straight stitches placed at regular intervals over rows of long horizontal stitches. Work small cross stitches over the points where two threads cross to hold the loose threads in place. The stitch can be adapted to achieve various results by crossing the straight stitches at random intervals or at different angles to each other. Different threads can be used for the straight and cross stitches or varieties of threads combined in one area.

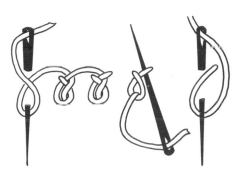

Rosette chain stitch

Bring the needle out to the right of the fabric and hold the thread down to the left. Then insert the needle just above the thread and bring it out a short distance below with the loop of thread beneath the needle. Pull the thread through and slip the needle upwards under the thread at the top of the stitch and through the fabric. Work the next stitch in the same way, as shown in the diagram.

Bokhara couching

A continuous thread is used for both the laid thread and tying stitches. Bring the needle up to one side of the area to be covered, take it across and insert it on the other side. Bring it up again a short distance back along the line of thread and just below it. Work small slanting stitches at regular intervals over the laid thread to secure it. Lay a second thread close to the first, stitching it in place as before.

EXPERIMENTS WITH STITCHES

Experiments will not only provide practical experience in the skills of stitchery but also in handling different combinations of fabric and thread. In this sense they can be compared with the painter's roughs and sketches.

It will become apparent that the relationship of fabric, thread and and stitch is of vital importance. Some threads are too fragile actually to stitch with, but can be couched in position with a stronger thread. Slubbed and uneven yarn does not pass through closely woven fabric, but can easily be couched to fabric with an even thread. Loosely spun and twisted threads, stranded silk and cotton give more successful results if worked in simple stitches, for example, straight and satin stitch, couching, chain, running and back stitch. Firmly twisted threads, coton perlé (pearl), coton-à-broder (embroidery), crochet cotton and wool, work well for couching and more complex stitches such as twisted chain, raised chain band and varieties of knot stitches. Many other threads, string, twine, raffia, knitting wools, may be couched; some will work well for a variety of stitches.

Experiments on a variety of fabrics can be very rewarding, since the effect of a stitch is influenced by the nature of the fabric. For example, if french knots are worked on to fabric with a highly pronounced structure such as tweed, stitch and fabric combine to create an integrated texture. The same knots appear to stand out from the surface of even, closely woven, smooth fabric. Stitches tend to be absorbed in richly textured fabric unless worked in thick contrasting threads.

Harmonious effects can be achieved by working stitches to reflect the texture and pattern qualities of fabrics. For example, running and back stitch and couching can be worked parallel to the pattern of striped woven or printed fabric. Contrasted textural effects can be achieved by working the same fabric with stripes or bands of knotted and twisted stitches (bullion knot, twisted chain, raised chain band). Greater contrast still results from working lines or bands of stitches at different angles to the stripe.

Texture and stitches
One of the most direct methods of effecting a change of texture and pattern in working embroidery is simply to couch threads and yarns to the surface of the fabric. Threads can be interlocked and overlapped in a virtually unlimited number of ways: laid and stitched in smooth parallel sequence or worked at random, couched to lie flat or allowed to loop and intertwine. Areas of fabric can be entirely covered with closely laid couched threads, or threads can be spaced out to allow the fabric to show through.

Cottage Garden (detail) by Glenys Crocker, 14 × 10 in. (355 × 255 mm), includes many of the stitches described on the preceding pages: straight and satin stitches, couched threads, french knot, detached chain stitch and cloud filling stitch. Stitches can be used to create entirely different moods. Compare the ordered style of this embroidery with the random scattering of stitches in the sampler overleaf.

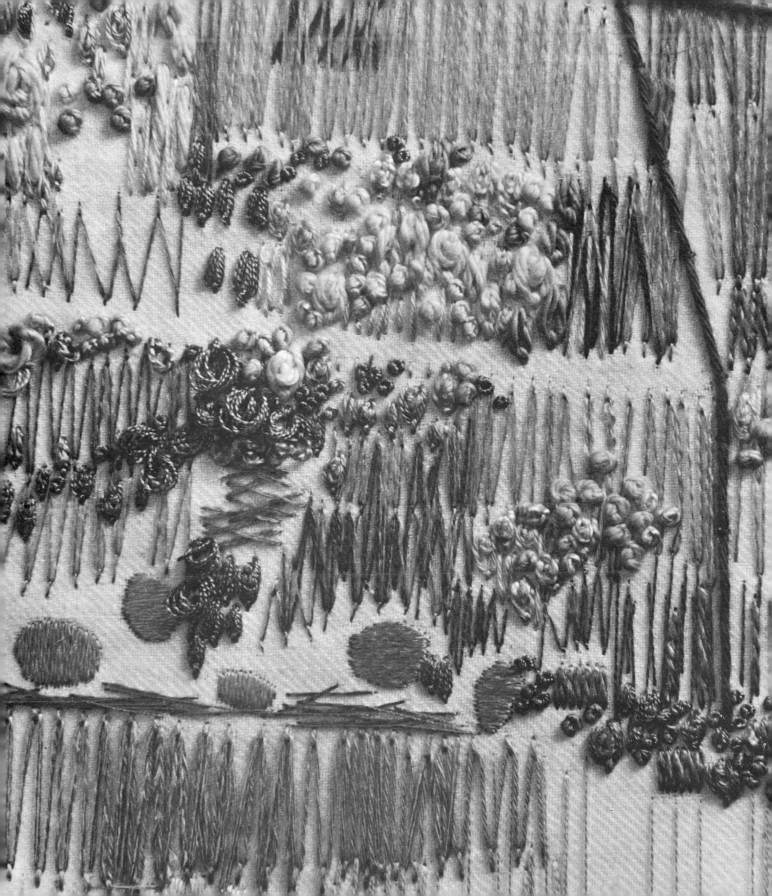

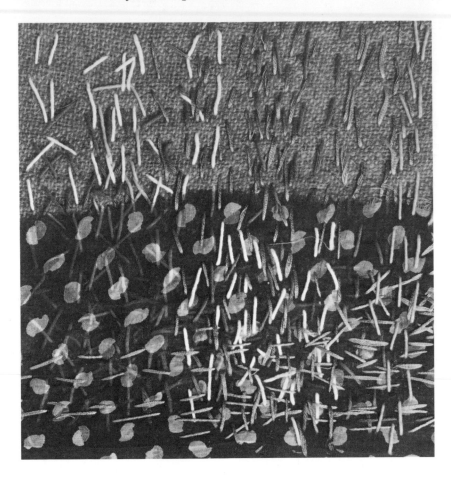

Sampler by Julia Jeffries, 9½ × 10 in. (240 × 255 mm). The stitches in this embroidery appear to integrate with the textured wool background and patterned cotton voile rather than standing out from the surface as in the samplers on page 89 and opposite. Straight stitches worked in stranded and soft cotton thread under and over the transparent voile result in an interesting shadow effect.

Other textures can be created by working different stitches together in one area. French knots and bullion knots work well with seeding. Areas of seeding can be effective when combined with larger straight stitches worked in different directions. The length of straight stitch can be varied, to combine successfully with lines of chain stitch, back and running stitch. Other effects can be obtained by changing the direction of the stitches. Overlapped straight stitch worked in a variety of threads produces superb textures, which can be further enriched with knotted and twisted stitches (detached chain, single twisted chain, french knots). Elaborate textures result from overlapped lines of cretan and herringbone stitch. Different threads can be used in working an area in any of these stitches. Experiment with similar coloured threads of different types and thicknesses and different coloured threads of the same type. The tone of the thread is frequently changed by light falling on the stitches: satin stitch worked in different directions is a good illustration of this. The change of tone is more obvious if shiny smooth threads (stranded cotton and silk) are used.

Scale of stitches

The scale of stitch has direct bearing on the finished embroidery. It is frequently necessary to alter the scale of stitch to suit particular designs. Rich textures and decorative patterns are obtained not only by using thicker threads, but also by enlarging the stitches in relation to the total shape and design of the embroidery. A relatively small stitch may have quite a definite and bold effect in a small design, while in a large embroidery it would seem almost to disappear. It is usually more successful to work small stitches in fine threads and large stitches in thicker threads. An embroidery carried out entirely with one stitch could combine different sizes of stitch to emphasize aspects of the pattern.

It is worth remembering, however, that some of the most pleasing results are obtained by arranging stitches in the simplest manner. The combination of too many different stitches of varying sizes often leads to confused pattern and design. The following suggestions outline some ways in which different sizes of stitch can be organized. Rows of stitches

Threads can be interlocked and over-lapped in a virtually unlimited number of ways. This sampler illustrates a few of the effects and combinations that can be achieved. From left to right: (*above*) straight stitches, french knots and seeding, straight stitches; (*below*) raised chain band, cretan stitch, detached chain and straight stitches. Before embarking on an embroidery, experiment with the stitches and threads you intend to use in order to discover the patterns and textural effects they create.

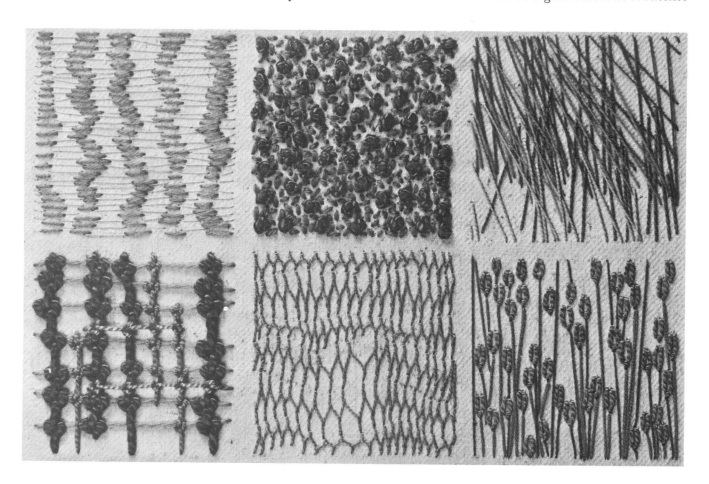

The scale of stitch is another important variable in an embroidery, especially if it is carried out entirely in one stitch. An effect of space and movement has been created in this design merely by varying the size and direction of the fly stitches that comprise it. Sampler by Anne Johnson, 6 × 9½ in. (150 × 241 mm).

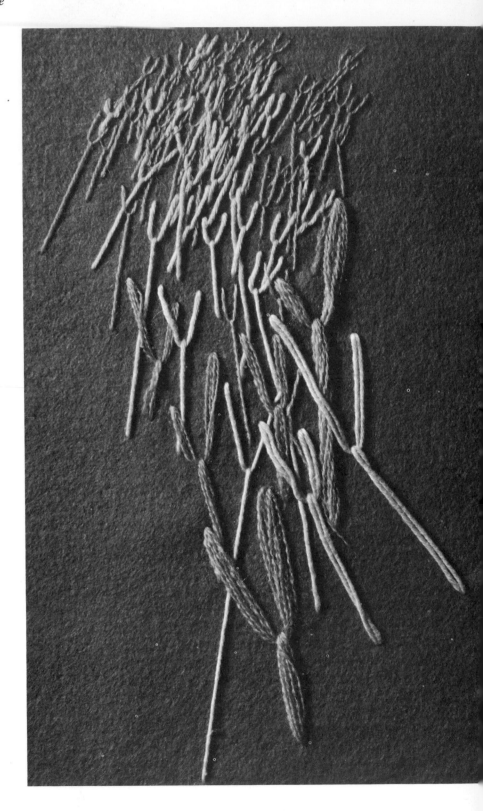

can be grouped together, working the first row in small stitches and gradually increasing the size in each subsequent row. Large and small, straight and curved rows of stitching can alternate with each other. Shapes worked in one size of stitch can alternate with others worked in different sizes of stitch. Shapes can be built up with large stitches in the centre and smaller ones at the edges.

Pattern with stitches

With ingenuity and a little forethought the embroiderer is able, using even only the basic stitches outlined above to work many decorative patterns, either with stitchery alone or combined with other methods.

Parallel and crossed lines of back, running, chain stitches and couched threads give different striped and checked patterns. Spaces between lines are increased or decreased to create larger or smaller pattern effects. The width of lines can be increased, to give added interest to a linear pattern, either by using thicker threads and larger stitches or by working several lines parallel to each other. Fluid patterns based on curved lines can be made with any of these stitches. Many stitches can be made to give all-over regular or random pattern effects. Wavy and straight lines of buttonhole, feather, herringbone and cretan stitch, worked closely together, will produce a variety of net-like patterns; the scale can be changed by altering the size of stitch and thread. Overlapped lines of these stitches result in dense, more solid pattern effects. Many stitches are worked to describe or fill shapes. Varieties of line and chain stitches are most commonly used to outline shapes, and lines of stitches grouped together and worked in any direction will create a solidly filled shape. Shape can also be described with net-like patterns produced with herringbone, cretan stitch, etc.

CANVAS WORK (NEEDLEPOINT)

This is a method in which an open-meshed canvas is completely filled in with stitches to form a close-knit firm surface. It is frequently mistakenly referred to as tapestry, probably because the finer types of canvas work are similar in appearance to woven tapestries.

Canvas work was used a great deal in the past to create a decorative, but close-knit and hard-wearing covering for items of furniture. Many experiments with new ways of working, introducing a variety of threads in different combinations, are giving canvas work a fresh and vital image.

Many canvas-work stitches are formed by working straight stitches either in a diagonal direction over the intersections of warp and weft threads of the canvas or horizontally or vertically to the threads.

Tent stitch or 'petit-point'

Tent stitch is a straight stitch worked diagonally over the intersection of one warp thread and one weft thread. The stitches may be worked in rows horizontally across the canvas. Usually the first row is worked from right to left across the canvas and the next row from left to right, the next row from right to left, and so on until the required area is covered. A more close-knit and firmer surface is achieved if the stitches are worked in diagonal rows across the canvas. This is a close filling stitch. Different coloured threads could be used to create a shaded effect. Matt and shiny threads could be combined in one area.

A Tent stitch
B Reverse tent stitch

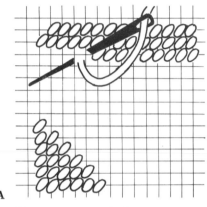

A

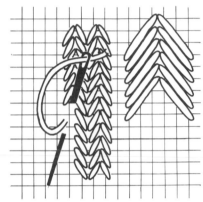

B

Reverse tent stitch

This is a variation of tent stitch, in which rows of diagonal stitches are worked in vertical rows on the canvas. In each row the direction of the diagonal is in reverse to the preceding row. Each stitch is worked over one vertical and across two horizontal threads of the canvas. The effect can be varied by working the stitches over more threads, for example, over three vertical and across four horizontal threads.

Cross stitch

This stitch can be made in two ways. (a) A diagonal straight stitch is taken over one intersection of threads, working from bottom right to top left, the second diagonal is taken from bottom left to top right. (b) A vertical stitch is taken over two threads of the canvas and a second stitch taken at a right angle across the first and over two threads of the canvas.

Upright Gobelin

This stitch consists of vertical straight stitches worked over two horizontal threads of the canvas. It can be worked over as many as four or five threads.

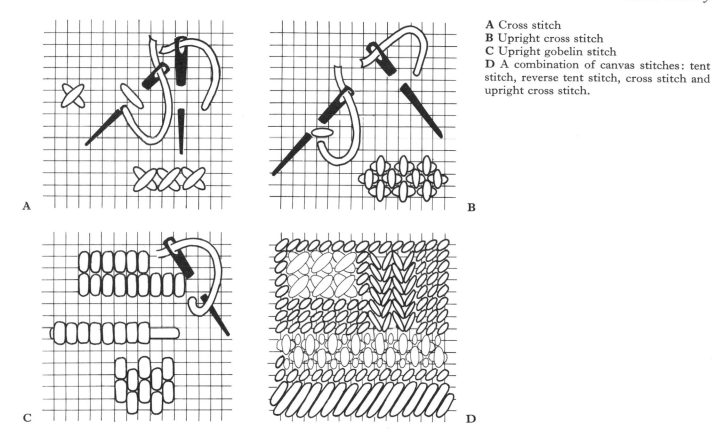

A Cross stitch
B Upright cross stitch
C Upright gobelin stitch
D A combination of canvas stitches: tent stitch, reverse tent stitch, cross stitch and upright cross stitch.

With these simple stitches many patterns and textures can be created. They can be organized into bands, grouped into units or blocks, and worked as lines between areas of different canvas stitches. Many different effects can be created simply by changing the number of threads of canvas over which the stitches are worked. A dictionary of stitches (see Bibliography, page 145) will provide more detailed instructions for creating specific patterns in canvas stitches. By introducing colour effects and by using a variety of threads canvas work can become an intriguing form of embroidery.

Canvas

There are two basic types, single-thread canvas, consisting of single threads equally spaced and woven vertically and horizontally; double-thread canvas consisting of pairs of two warp threads and two weft threads. Both fine and coarse canvases are manufactured, these qualities being determined by the number of threads to the inch. Single canvas is obtainable in a range of 10 to 28 threads per inch. For the first experiment a coarse canvas is easier to work on. Rug canvas could be used for large, bolder designs.

Detail of canvas work by Becky Mullins, 8 × 6 in. (203 × 150 mm). The stitches used in canvas work are very simple but they need not confine the embroiderer to the simple repeat patterns suggested by their geometric form. Many patterns and textural effects can be created by varying the number of threads of canvas over which the stitches are worked (see also page 25). Further variations can be introduced by leaving areas of the canvas uncovered or by threading ribbon, tape, string, strips of leather or fabric into it.

It is advisable to use a frame to prevent the canvas from pulling out of shape during the working process. Smaller pieces can be mounted on to ring frames, larger pieces on slate frames. Mount the canvas according to the instructions on page 31. Before mounting the canvas, the two side edges must be bound with wide tape to strengthen them and produce a firm edge for the lacing threads.

The design can be marked on the canvas in one of three ways. (a) Draw a bold outline on paper with a black waterproof ink or felt-tipped pen. Place the drawing beneath the canvas and tack (baste) or pin the two together. The outline will show through the mesh and can be used as a guide for tracing the design on to the canvas. (b) Work the design out on graph paper which has the same number of squares to the inch as the canvas. Work the canvas by the counting method, using the graph as a guide. (c) Tack the design directly on the canvas.

Threads

The choice of threads depends to a large extent on the type of canvas used. The structure of a fine canvas would be deformed by forcing thick thread through it. Thick threads are necessary for coarse canvas which is to be closely covered with stitches. Apart from these considerations many types of threads and yarns may be used. Tapestry and crewel wool are hard-wearing threads manufactured especially for canvas work. Crewel wool is a fine 2-ply wool, tapestry wool a thicker 4-ply wool. When designing for canvas work it is worth considering the contrasting effects achieved with matt and shiny threads. Coton perlé (pearl cotton), raffia, silk, plastic string, all add to the variety of contrasting effects. It is even possible to use other materials on coarse canvas as well as the normal rug and weaving wools. Ribbon, tape, string, strips of leather and fabric can be used to introduce an interesting range of effects; they can also be used in conjunction with normal threads.

8 Machine embroidery

Most modern domestic machines are electrically driven and designed to work embroidered patterns and decoration, as well as plain sewing.

Zigzag machines produced for the domestic market are designed to sew both straight and zigzag stitches. The width of the zigzag stitch varies with different makes of machine, some giving only a narrow width and others up to almost a quarter of an inch (3 mm). The width and length of stitches can be varied within the limits of the machine. The length of stitch lever can be set to give very close zigzag stitch, which resembles satin stitch.

Minimatic and fully automatic are swing-needle machines, which will sew both straight and zigzag stitch. Pattern discs which produce embroidery patterns are built into the structure of the machine which is

Compare machine-embroidered straight stitches and whipped-cord effects with the hand-embroidered examples on pages 105 and 106. Guide the fabric fairly quickly under the needle and keep the tension at normal to produce small, even, controlled stitches that can be closely worked and overlapped to create a pattern of curved shapes. Free machine embroidery, Goldsmiths' College, School of Art, London, 6 × 7½ in. (150 × 190 mm).

designed for this purpose. Minimatic machines usually produce no more than four or five patterns but fully automatic machines are normally capable of producing up to twenty.

Machines which have a lever for lowering the feed are more efficient and easier to use than those with a cover plate to place over the feed. Free embroidery is worked by removing the presser foot and lowering or covering the feed. The fabric is moved under the needle by the operator.

Almost any fabric, whether natural or synthetic, can be used for machine embroidery. It is wise to avoid very closely woven and harsh fabrics such as cotton, poplin and sailcloth, which cause friction and often lead to the breaking of the top thread during the stitching process. Soft, pliable fabrics, varieties of cotton, net, lawn, calico (muslin), denim, corduroy and velvet, soft woollen fabrics, flannel, crêpe, georgette and jersey, silk organdie, wild silk, even-weave linen, crash and scrim; nylon, Terylene or polyester, rayon, satin and grosgrain; P.V.C. and soft plastic sheeting, all work successfully with machine embroidery. Some fabrics worked with the presser foot on may require support to prevent them puckering during the stitching process (see page 118).

Machine embroidery threads No. 30 and No. 50 are the most frequently used. Mercerized cotton No. 60 is equivalent in thickness to No. 30 machine embroidery cotton and adapts well to working free embroidery and embroidery with the presser foot on. Thicker threads, coton perlé, knitting wool, rug wool and even thin cords can be couched to fabric with straight and zigzag stitch.

FREE MACHINE EMBROIDERY

This is worked with the presser foot removed and the feed lowered or covered. When the presser foot is removed no pressure is exerted to hold the fabric flat on the machine. To counteract this, fabric must be stretched taut over a ring frame, preferably a metal one, but a wooden one is suitable.

First disengage the pattern lever on automatic pattern machines. Thread the machine with machine embroidery or mercerized cotton. Set the tension to normal and work a test piece of straight stitches. The tension may have to be altered slightly at a later stage.

Place the fabric, in its frame with right side upwards, flat on the bed of the machine, under the needle. Then lower the presser bar, even though the presser foot has been removed. If it is not lowered, there will be no tension on the top thread and the bottom thread will not be drawn upwards. Instead it will wrap round the race causing the mechanism to jam. With the top thread held in the left hand, lower the needle

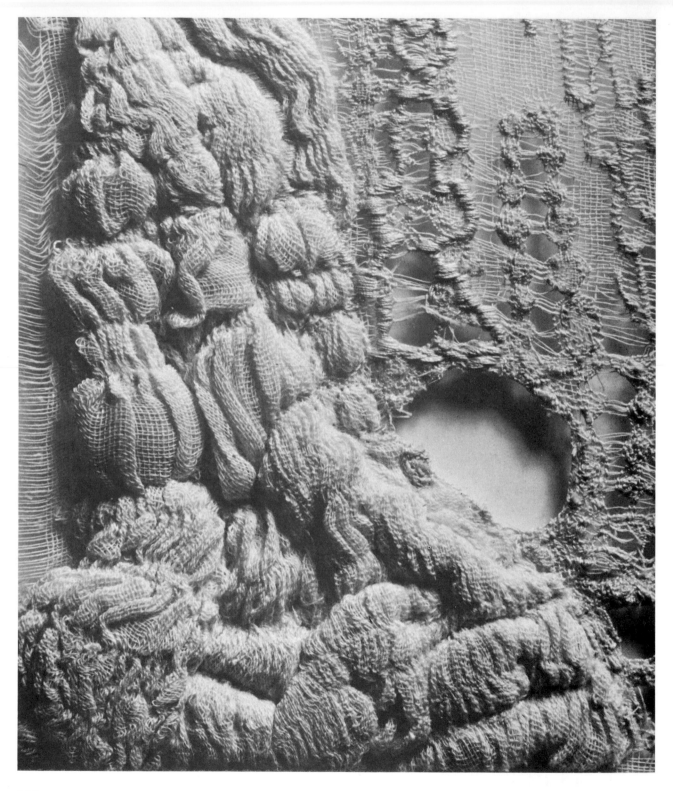

Free machine embroidery by Sue Moss, 6 × 7½ in. (150 × 190 mm). Machine-stitched drawn thread and cutwork on loosely woven cotton (the backing from Terylene wadding) have been combined with padded and stuffed techniques to achieve a balance between solid and net-like areas. Almost any fabric, whether natural or synthetic, is suitable for machine embroidery and it can be employed in many of the techniques discussed in chapters 4, 5 and 6.

into the fabric by turning the wheel with the right hand. This action draws the bottom thread up through to the right side of the fabric. Holding both threads in the left hand, work a few stitches by guiding the ring frame under the needle. Proceed with stitching, using both hands to guide the fabric.

The length of stitch will depend on how fast the fabric is guided under the needle in relation to the speed of the machine, for the length of stitch lever does not function when the feed is lowered and the presser foot removed. Fabric can be moved in any direction, allowing different arrangements of curved, straight and crossed lines of stitching to be worked. With some practice it is possible to achieve considerable control, so that small, intricate patterns and curved lines can be as easily worked as large patterns and flowing curves.

Different effects can be achieved in working free machine embroidery by altering the tension when working straight stitches and by setting the machine for zigzag stitch.

A whipped cord effect is obtained by tightening the top tension and loosening the bottom tension. (Alterations to the bottom tension are made by turning the tension screw which holds the tension band on the bobbin case. It is turned anti-clockwise to loosen the tension and clockwise to tighten.) Set the machine for straight stitch. Guide the fabric slowly under the needle to obtain a close corded effect.

For zigzag stitch, set the machine as for free embroidery, but with the width of stitch lever set for zigzag. Again, the length of stitch is determined by the speed of the fabric passing under the needle. If the fabric is moved slowly, zigzag builds up into satin stitch. Free machine embroidery using zigzag stitching can be very effective if worked on loosely woven fabric such as linen and scrim. Set the tension slightly tighter than normal and thread the machine top and bottom with machine embroidery or mercerized cotton. Unravel some of the warp or weft threads of the fabric and either cut them away or catch them in the stitching. The result is similar to hand drawn thread work, consisting of thick bands of stitching with open spaces between. Lacy effects produced by cutting shapes out of fabric and working the empty space with machine embroidery are described in the section on cutwork (page 54).

MACHINE EMBROIDERY WITH THE PRESSER FOOT IN POSITION

The machine is used with the presser foot in position for quilting, appliqué, crazy patchwork and decorative, automatic patterns. It is also used in couching thick and thin threads to the surface of fabric.

Landscape by Judith Standeven, 10 × 6½ in. (255 × 165 mm). Appliqué embroidered with flowing lines of machine stitches – straight, whipped and zigzag stitches worked with the presser foot removed – that pick out and repeat the patterns of the fabrics used and add an interesting textural contrast.

Embroidery produced in this way is generally not as fluid as free embroidery for it is only possible to follow gentle curves and straight lines.

Raise the feed and thread the machine, top and bottom, with machine embroidery or mercerized cotton. The top tension should be slightly looser than normal, to ensure that the threads interlock on the back of the fabric. To prevent single layers of fabric from puckering during the stitching process, drafting or cutting paper, thin iron-on Vilene (Pellon) or vanishing muslin can be used as a support. Drafting paper is slipped under the fabric just before stitching and torn away when the embroidery is complete. Iron-on Vilene is fixed to the fabric before stitching and remains in position when the work is finished. Vanishing muslin must be tacked or basted on before stitching and removed with a hot iron. It is not necessary to use any of these supports when working on P.V.C. (sheet plastic), thicker plastics and leather.

Straight, zigzag stitch and automatic patterns can all be used in a design. The length of straight stitch and the length and width of zigzag stitch can be altered to give different effects. The length of stitch lever is positioned just before zero to obtain satin stitch. Lines of straight zigzag and satin stitch could be arranged in sequence to achieve striped patterns; checked and squared patterns are made by crossing lines of stitching. Richly worked shapes can be achieved by covering areas of the fabric with closely arranged lines of stitching. Stitched lines can be worked horizontally, vertically and diagonally to the shape. Spaces between stitched lines can be varied.

9 Additional materials

Anything that can be held in position with threads can be used with embroidery, to create contrasts of texture and to add emphasis to a design.

BEADS AND SEQUINS

There is a profusion of beads, sequins and imitation jewels on the market today. Clear, opaque and translucent glass (and plastic) beads with plain or faceted surfaces can be obtained in a variety of colours and sizes. There is a more limited range of square and round wooden beads, natural or stained. Very small and quite large sequins are manufactured in different colours.

In normal use beads, sequins and jewels are stitched to fabric with an ordinary strong sewing cotton or silk thread. A fine smooth embroidery thread (coton-à-broder) can be substituted for sewing larger beads. Very large ones can be sewn with any strong thread; really thick threads can be used if they will pass through the bead hole and the fabric easily. They are usually sewn close and firm to the fabric, but beads can be slipped on to a knotted thread and attached to the fabric as a kind of fringe. The thread used for this should be reasonably strong and smooth.

Beads, sequins and jewels should be used with discretion if garish and crude effects are to be avoided. They can be mixed in with stitches to bring added contrasts of texture and emphasis to parts of a design. Small beads, etc., are usually best grouped together.

RIBBON, BRAID AND CORD

Rayon ribbon of plain or ribbed weave and satin ribbon are obtainable in different widths and colours. Velvet ribbon seems to be manufactured in a greater variety of colours than any other type of ribbon. It is made in a range of widths from $\frac{1}{4}$ in. (6 mm) up to 2 to 3 in. (50 to 75 mm). Patterned, printed, woven and machine-stitched ribbons, tape, seam binding and any other types of ribbons may be incorporated into embroidery. Ribbon and braid can be applied flat to fabric or pleated and gathered into frills and ruffs. Very wide ribbon could be cut into shapes and used for patchwork and appliqué.

Cords, made of rayon, gold and silver threads, synthetic threads, nylon, lurex and plastic are manufactured in several thicknesses. Varieties of cord, braid and fringing produced for furnishing and upholstery may also be used. They are couched down or sewn with machine or hand stitches to fabrics.

SKINS AND LEATHER

Skins and leather (crocodile skin, suede, gold and silver kid) can be cut easily and applied to the surface of fabric or used for patchwork. Besides their beautiful surface pattern and texture, they have the added advantage of not fraying. They can be stitched in position with small straight stitches (machine straight stitch or zigzag stitch) worked over the edge. Shapes can be padded by stitching a pad of felt to the embroidery and then smoothing the skin or leather over it and securing with small straight stitches as already described (page 94). Leather can be cut and stitched in the same way as fabric patchwork; it is usually sufficiently firm to make the use of backing paper patterns unnecessary. A gloving needle is useful for the stitching process. It has a triangular-cut point which enables it to pass through leather easily. A fine, twisted silk thread of strong quality is used for stitching gold and silver kid. This type of thread is also the most suitable for other leathers and skins, but a normal good quality sewing thread is adequate.

SYNTHETIC MATERIALS

Transparent polythene sheeting is manufactured in different weights (thicknesses). Very light (thin) types are not suitable for stitchery as they are liable to tear during the stitching process. Heavier (thicker) polythene can be worked with machine or hand stitches. One of the fascinating effects of stitching through polythene and transparent plastic is that the back of the work is visible from the right side. Polythene shows the effect to greater advantage than transparent coloured plastic. Shadow quilting and machine embroidery give successful results worked in transparent plastic and polythene. Many colours of semi-transparent acetate are available, and though acetate is not sufficiently flexible for working patchwork, quilting, etc., it is easily cut and applied to flat surfaces of fabric. It can be stitched in a similar way to sequins. Before stitching, pierce small holes with a needle near the edges of the shape. Needle and thread should then pass easily through

One of the fascinating effects of working embroidery on transparent plastic is that the backs of the stitches are visible from the right side. This can create a feeling of depth as compared with the flatness of the same stitches worked on opaque fabric; a contrast which has been skilfully employed in this work. A sheet of plastic embroidered with undulating waves of straight stitches has been mounted in front of fabric both hand painted and stitched with similar shapes. *Waves*, Goldsmiths' College, School of Art, London, $8\frac{1}{2} \times 8\frac{1}{2}$ in. (216 × 216 mm).

the fabric and the holes. Small straight stitches worked through the holes and over the edges of the shape should be sufficiently strong to keep the acetate in position. Embroidered designs can be carried out entirely in these materials or in a mixture of woven fabrics, plastic and polythene sheeting and P.V.C.

10 Finishing and presentation

A successfully completed and well-presented piece of work provides its own reward, and the effect of a well-planned embroidery, executed with consideration and care, can be ruined by a lack of attention to the finish and mode of presentation.

Often an embroidery needs some neatening before it can be stretched, mounted and framed or made up into a functional item. Remove loose ends of thread and visible tacking (basting) stitches. Take through ends of thread and oversew to the back of the work. Cut off short ends close to the fabric.

Embroidery worked on a frame should remain flat and unwrinkled, but if slight puckers occur, they can be removed by shrinking the material. Place the work face downwards over a soft blanket, damp the back and press with a hot iron using a pressing cloth. If the puckering is pronounced the work can be damp-stretched.

DAMP-STRETCHING EMBROIDERY

Embroidery worked without a frame is likely to become creased and puckered. These faults can be corrected by damp-stretching the piece before finishing and lining the work. Place several sheets of blotting paper on a flat wooden board, to cover an area slightly larger than the embroidery, and dampen it with clean water. Place the embroidery right side upwards on the damp blotting paper and pin it to the board through the paper using rust-proof drawing pins (thumb tacks). Insert the drawing pins at intervals of 1 in. (25 mm) and at least 1 in. (25 mm) from the edge of the embroidery through the turning allowance. Pin the centre of each side first. Then pin along one edge working from the centre outwards to the corners. Next, pin the opposite side. While inserting the pins, pull the fabric gently but firmly until it is stretched taut on the board. Pin the two remaining sides as before. Make sure that the fabric is pulled straight with the grain (warp and weft threads square with each other).

Thick fabric or embroidery consisting of several layers of fabric may be dampened on the surface once it has been stretched. Cover the stretched fabric with a sheet of paper and leave for twenty-four hours or until it is absolutely dry.

MOUNTING EMBROIDERIES AND SAMPLERS

Small pieces of work can be stretched over card and mounted in a window frame of card. Mounting card (matting board) is available in a variety of colours and should be selected carefully in relationship to the colour scheme of the embroidery. Neutral colours such as white and grey show most colour schemes to advantage. Coloured mounts should not overpower or lessen the intensity of the colours of the embroidery. Samplers and experimental pieces can be stretched and mounted on card and kept in a folio. Small embroideries can be stretched and mounted on card and then framed. Many embroiderers prefer to use the services of a professional frame-maker for this purpose. Really good frames can be extremely difficult to make without the proper tools and equipment.

For stretching embroidery over card it is advisable to use reasonably thick card, which will not buckle when fabric is laced over it. Cut a piece of card to the size of the embroidery, allowing an extra $\frac{1}{2}$ in. (12 mm) on all sides for the overlap of the window frame. Allow only $\frac{1}{4}$ in. (6 mm) if the embroidery is to be framed with wood or metal frames, without a card mount (surround): this is sufficient to allow for the overlap of the frame. Place the embroidery face downwards on a flat surface and position the card over it. Fold the turning allowance down over the back of the card and lace the edges together with a long herring-bone stitch. Use a strong thread such as buttonhole twist or fine string for the lacing, which must be pulled tight in order to stretch the fabric firmly over the card.

To mount the embroidery, cut a piece of card large enough to allow for a window frame to fit the mounted embroidery. For example, the size of card for an embroidery 6×8 in. (150×200 mm) with a margin of 3 in. (75 mm) would be 12×14 in. (300×350 mm). Always cut card with a sharp knife, as it is virtually impossible to achieve a clean straight cut edge with scissors. Using a hard pencil, mark the size of the window frame lightly on the card. In the example given above it would be 3 in. (75 mm) in from the edges of the card. Cut out the shape of the window frame with a steel ruler and sharp knife (Stanley knife or matt knife). Cut with the ruler covering the surround: this should prevent the card being damaged if the knife slips. Place the card mount over the embroidery, securing the edges on the back of the card with Sellotape (Scotch tape). Embroidery worked on thick heavy fabric requires a stronger support. Hardboard $\frac{1}{4}$ in. (6 mm) thick will provide adequate support and can be used for stretching embroideries up to 24 in. (600 mm) square. Card window frames are not suitable for embroideries stretched over hardboard. The card can be easily damaged by the weight and rigidity of the hardboard.

STRETCHING EMBROIDERY ON RIGID WOODEN FRAMES

Large stretched embroideries require a strong rigid support to keep the fabric in firm even tension. Painters' canvas stretchers may be used for this purpose and can be bought in sections to be assembled at home. Alternatively, rigid wooden frames can be made (see page 27) but they should be strong and firm. The joints could be glued as well as nailed or screwed together. Triangular-shaped pieces of hardboard can be tacked across the corners, on the back of the frame, to give additional strength and rigidity. Leave a space of at least 1 in. (25 mm) between the outer edge of the frame and the pieces of hardboard. The corners of the fabric can be tacked to this area to neaten the back of the work.

When stretching the embroidery, first mark the centre of each side on the back of the frame. Mark the centre of each side of the embroidery and place these marks to correspond with the centres of the matching sides of the frame. Pin temporarily with drawing pins (thumb tacks), working along one side from the centre outwards to the corners. Then pin the opposite side, pulling the embroidery firmly. The two remaining sides are pinned as before. The embroidery should be taut with the grain of fabric straight and square with the frame. Fold the corners neatly, cutting away surplus bulk. The embroidery is attached permanently with a staple gun or tacks and the drawing pins removed. A neater finish is achieved if the work is stretched right over the frame and tacked to the back.

The stretched panel can be neatened with a piece of calico (muslin) or cotton sheeting sewn to the back of the work. The edges of the panel may be left plain or finished with metal strips or wood battens which can be stained or painted to match the colour scheme of the embroidery. These can be fixed to the stretcher with screws, countersunk for a neat finish. Aluminium strips can be bought in various widths and, like wood, can be screwed to the frame. Both wood and metal strips protect the edges of the embroidery as well as providing a neat finish to the work.

LININGS

Linings are necessary for neatening and protecting the back of embroideries, hangings in particular. They also provide additional firmness which helps to preserve the shape when the embroidery is hung. Lining fabrics should be strong and firm. A fabric similar to that used for the background of the embroidery may be used. Curtain lining, cotton sheeting or calico are also suitable.

Interline the embroidery first (see opposite), or if an interlining is not being used, fold the turning allowance of the embroidery down to the wrong side. Pin then tack or baste in position making sure that the corners are quite square and the edges straight.

Cut the lining to the size of the embroidery including an extra 1 in. (25 mm) on all sides for a turning allowance. Mark the centre of each edge on both the embroidery and the lining with pins. Fold the turning allowance, plus an extra $\frac{1}{4}$ in. (6 mm), of the lining down to the wrong side. Pin and tack, making sure that the edges are quite straight. The lining should now be $\frac{1}{2}$ in. (12 mm) smaller all round than the embroidery and this should prevent it showing if it should shift when the embroidery is hung. Then place the embroidery right side downwards on a flat clean surface. Place the lining on top of it with the turning allowance face downwards. Pin down the centre. Then pin and tack the lining to the embroidery. Tack lines at intervals of 4 to 6 in. (100 to 150 mm) down the length and across the shape. Both lining and embroidery should be smooth and free from wrinkles. Tack around the edge of the lining. At this point the embroidery can be held or hung up to check that the lining is not pulled anywhere. Finally sew the folded edge of the lining to the embroidery with slip stitch. The stitching should be worked through the fold of the turning allowance of the embroidery and should not be visible on the right side of the work.

INTERLININGS

These are used to give additional body and crispness to hangings and banners, for example. Like linings they help to preserve the shape of the embroidery when it is hung. Interlining may not be necessary if the embroidery has been worked on a firm, strong fabric with an equally firm backing material. An ordinary non-woven interlining such as Vilene or Pellon (not iron-on) can be used for small embroideries. Crisp, firm wool interlining or a reasonably firm calico (muslin) can be used for interlining larger work.

Cut the interlining on the straight grain to the exact size of the embroidery. Place the embroidery face downwards on a clean flat surface, place the interlining on it and pin in position. Sew the two fabrics together with vertical and horizontal tacked lines through the centre of the shape. Work lines of tacking at intervals of 4 to 6 in. (100 to 150 mm) across and down the length of the shape. Make sure that both grains are straight with each other and both fabrics flat and unwrinkled. Fold the turning allowance on all sides down on to the interlining and pin and tack. Make neat, flat folds at the corners, which should be exactly square. Sew the edges of the turning allowance to the interlining with herringbone stitch using a normal sewing cotton. The method for adding interlinings to hangings mounted directly on battens or rods is slightly different.

SUPPORTS FOR HANGINGS AND BANNERS

Flat battens or rods of wood or metal can be used for hanging unframed embroidery; at the same time, of course, they preserve its shape. They can be inserted through hems at the top and bottom of the hangings, inserted in channels of fabric sewn to the back of the hanging (in which case they are not visible on the front of the work) or used with tabs to provide a visible means of support. Each method produces successful results and it is simply a question of choosing the one which will best complement and enhance the work.

Wooden battens can be obtained in various widths of different thicknesses. Battens 1 in. (25 mm) wide and $\frac{1}{4}$ or $\frac{1}{2}$ in. (6 or 12 mm) thick provide adequate support for most sizes of embroidery. If the hanging is rather heavy, metal strips (brass, steel or aluminium) $\frac{1}{8}$ in. (3 mm) thick can be used instead. Narrow wooden dowel rods are only suitable for lightweight embroidery. Large and heavy work must be supported on thick rods. Copper, brass and chrome rods of different diameters can be bought, although they are more expensive than the wooden ones. Wooden battens and rods could be stained or painted to match or tone with the colour scheme of the embroidery.

Mounting embroidery on battens or rods

Fold the turning allowances of the two vertical edges down on to the wrong side of the embroidery and pin and tack. Fold a small part of the turning allowance on the top edge down to the wrong side of the fabric and tack. Then fold the rest of the turning allowance down on to the wrong side of the embroidery, making a hem of sufficient depth to allow the batten or rod to be slipped through it. Pin and tack the hem in place. Using normal sewing cotton, work a line of straight machine stitch or double running stitch close to the folded edge of the hem. Only a slight ridge will show if the hem is deeper than the width of the batten or rod. Make a second hem on the bottom edge of the hanging. The hanging can be lined in the normal way, except that the lining is sewn just over the folded edge of the top and bottom hems.

Hangings made up with an interlining and mounted directly on battens or rods require a slightly different working method. The width of the interlining should be equal to the width of the embroidery, i.e., not including the turning allowance. Cut the interlining to the length of the embroidery, including the turning allowance, and tack in the normal way. Then fold the turning allowance of the two vertical sides down on

Detail of a three-dimensional landscape picture by Carol Blackburn, $43\frac{1}{2} \times 43\frac{1}{2} \times 4\frac{3}{4}$ in. (1105 × 1105 × 120 mm). Motifs of crochet on a smocking background. Courtesy of the Crafts Advisory Committee.

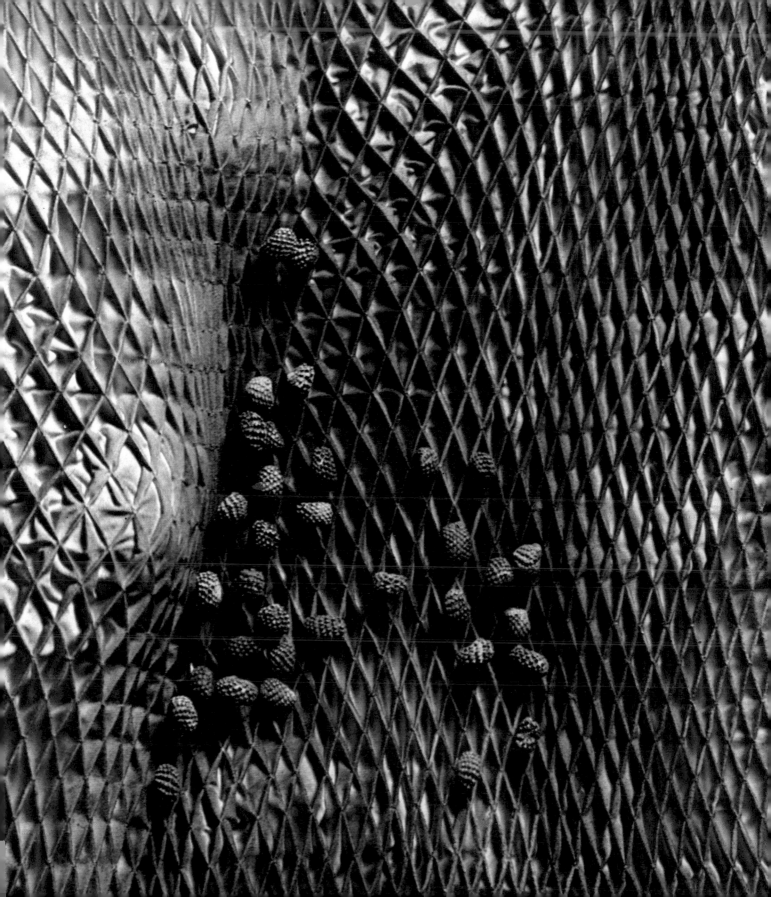

Sunset over St Ouen by Anne Spence, 6 × 10 in. (150 × 255 mm). Embroidery on fabric which has been previously hand painted, like a watercolour, with washes of water-based dyes. The painting is an integral part of the design; both stitches and background act as a foil for each other. If the painting could stand alone, then the embroidery would be only an unnecessary embellishment.

to the interlining. Tack and sew in the usual way. Make hems including the edges of the interlining on both the top and bottom edges of the hanging. The hanging can then be lined and rods slipped through the hems.

Battens are usually longer than the width of the hanging and the protruding sections of the rods can rest on hooks or nails in a wall. Alternatively the work can be hung by means of cord fixed at either end of the batten.

Channels

The fabric to make the channel is sewn to the lining before the lining is stitched to the embroidery. The same type of fabric is used for the lining and the channel. Before making the channel, fold the turning allowance on the lining to the wrong side of the fabric and tack. If an interlining is necessary, mount the embroidery over this in the normal way. Make sure that all edges are straight and the corners exactly square.

Cut a strip of fabric equal to the width of the hanging. The width of the strip should allow for the width and thickness of the batten and should include an extra $\frac{1}{2}$ in. (12 mm) on each side for a turning allowance. Then fold the turning allowance on all sides to the wrong side of the fabric and tack. Tack a line on the right side of the lining, parallel to and about $\frac{3}{4}$ to 1 in. (18 to 25 mm) away from the top edge. Tack a second line parallel to the first. Leave sufficient distance between the lines to allow for the width of the batten, $1\frac{1}{4}$ in. (30 mm) for a batten 1 in. (25 mm) wide. Place the strip with the turning face downwards on the lining, matching the long sides to the tacked lines. Pin and tack the strip in position. The strip should not lie flat on the lining, as it should be wider than the distance between the lines. The strip is finally attached with lines of machine straight stitch or small back stitches worked close to the turned edges of the strip. Both ends are left open. A second channel may be added to the bottom of the lining. The lining is then attached to the embroidery in the normal way.

Tabs

Hangings can be supported on rods or battens by means of tabs inserted and sewn between the embroidery and the lining. Tabs are usually made of the same fabric as the embroidery, but a different fabric may be used. They should always be interlined. Whatever size tab you are making, always allow an extra $\frac{1}{2}$ in. (12 mm) on each of the vertical sides for a turning allowance, and include at least $\frac{3}{4}$ in. (18 mm) extra on both ends of the tab to be inserted between the embroidery and the lining.

To make a tab 1 in. wide by 2 in. long (25 × 50 mm) cut two strips

$2 \times 6\frac{1}{2}$ in. (50×165 mm) on the straight grain of the fabric. These measurements include turning allowances and $\frac{3}{4}$ in. (18 mm) at either end for inserting between the lining and the embroidery.

Place the interlining on the wrong side of one of the strips of fabric and tack in position. Turn the allowance down on to the interlining and pin and tack. Make neat flat corners. Sew the edges of the turning allowance to the interlining with herringbone stitch (page 99) using a normal sewing cotton. Fold the turning allowance of the second strip down to the wrong side of the fabric and tack. Make the lining slightly smaller than the first strip. Place the lining, with turned edges facing inwards, on to the interlined strip; pin and tack in position. Finally slip stitch the folded edges of the lining to the interlined strip.

To attach the tab to the hanging, fold the tab in half (horizontally) and place the ends over the edge of the hanging on the wrong side of the work. About $\frac{3}{4}$ in. (18 mm) of the tab should lie on the hanging. Stitch the tab to the interlining of the embroidery with small herringbone stitches. Use a No. 40 sewing cotton. Tack the lining to the hanging, covering the ends of the tabs, then stitch it in the normal way. To ensure that the tabs are held firmly, work a line of straight machine stitching or back stitch close to the edge of the hanging through the lining, tabs and embroidery.

11 Allied crafts

Although the essence of embroidery is the manipulation of fabric and thread, usually conceived as the application of thread to fabric and fabric to fabric, allied crafts perform a vital, if supporting, role. The crafts of woven and printed textile, of knitting, crochet and macramé are directly linked to embroidery through the common factor of fabric and thread. It seems a natural progression, in view of this link, for the embroiderer to experiment with these crafts, combining and mixing them with the techniques of embroidery to achieve a fresh and vital quality.

When planning a design to be carried out in a mixture of techniques, for example, printing, embroidery or embroidery/weaving, both should be considered as necessary and integral parts of the whole design. Whether one technique plays the major role in the design or whether both are equally important, each should act as a foil for the other. If the design of a printed or woven fabric can stand successfully alone, embroidery would only be an unnecessary and superficial embellishment.

Printing and weaving can be developed into highly creative art forms. Printing techniques such as block and screen printing are relatively complicated and require more specialized equipment. Woven fabrics created on sophisticated looms also involve more complex technical processes. Only basic principles and simple methods for creating woven and patterned fabric will be described here. The methods include weaving on a frame loom, tie dyeing, batik, freehand painting of dyes and drawing with pastel dyes. Some reference to the use of knitted fabrics, crochet and macramé with embroidery will also be made.

WEAVING ON A FRAME LOOM

The basic principle of weaving is the interlacing of threads over and under each other to create a fabric. In their simplest form woven fabrics consist of two series of threads: warp and weft. Warp threads run parallel to the length of the fabric and are the basic structure on which the fabric is formed. Weft threads interlace with the warp threads across the width of the fabric. During the construction of a fabric, a loom is required to hold the warp threads under tension.

Simple woven fabrics can be constructed on a primitive type of loom, consisting of a rigid wooden frame with nails inserted in top and bottom edges. A frame can be made according to the directions on page 27, but using $1\frac{1}{2} \times 2$ in. (38×50 mm) strips of wood. Strengthen the frame with corner plates screwed to the inside corners. For the first experiments a frame 16×18 in. (400×450 mm) would be suitable, allowing for the weaving of pieces up to 12×14 in. (300×350 mm). Larger frames over 5 ft (1.525 metres) square should be constructed of 2×2 in. (50×50 mm) wood. To insert the nails, place the frame on a flat surface and mark the centre of the uppermost side on the top and bottom struts of the frame. Mark lines at intervals of $\frac{3}{8}$ in. (9 mm) to each side of the centre, leaving 2 in. (50 mm) clear at the ends of each strut. Hammer $\frac{3}{4}$ in. (18 mm) flat-headed nails at each marked interval.

Using a ball of thread, attach a continuous warp to the loom. Any type of thread may be used, cotton, silk, wool, linen or synthetic, so long as it is strong enough not to break under tension. Knobbly, slubbed and hairy threads are more suitable for the weft. With the frame loom placed on a flat surface, tie one end of the thread to the first nail on the top edge of the frame. Carry the thread across and round the outside of the first and second nails on the bottom edge. Take the threads across and round the second and third nails on the top edge. The thread is then taken down round the third and fourth nails on the opposite edge. Continue warping in this way, taking the thread round two nails before crossing to the other side. Finish off by tying the thread to a nail on the bottom edge of the frame. The warp should not be slack.

The warp can now be laced with the weft threads. This work may be done with the fingers, although it may be rather difficult when warp threads lie close together. An alternative is to use a bodkin (a long blunt implement used for threading tape and elastic). Weaving is much easier if weft threads are wound on to shuttles. A simple shuttle can be made from a small wood lath 6 to 12 in. (150 to 300 mm) long. Cut a deep notch at either end of the lath and smooth down with sandpaper (glasspaper).

Working from right to left weave the weft thread under and over alternating threads of the warp. Return the thread to the other side of the work in the same way. If the first row of the weft finished under the last warp thread, the second row is started with weft thread over the last warp. Continue in this way until the required amount of fabric has been woven.

Shed sticks make the process easier still. Their function is to lift alternate warp threads, creating a space, or shed, through which a shuttle can be passed. They are also used to push the weft into place.

Shed sticks can be made from $\frac{1}{8} \times 1$ in. (3×25 mm) wood laths. Sticks should be slightly longer than the width of the frame, as they

Weaving and embroidery, $5\frac{1}{2} \times 9\frac{1}{2}$ in. (140 × 240 mm), combined in a perfectly balanced design, both crafts being a necessary part of the whole. The weaving was done on the frame loom described on pages 131–2.

rest on top of it. The ends can be rounded off and smoothed down with sandpaper.

Three shed sticks will be required in working the following method. One stick is inserted under and over alternating warp threads and placed close to the bottom edge of the frame. Its function is to hold the threads in firm tension and also to ensure that adequate thread is left for tying and neatening when the weaving is complete. The two other sticks are used for obtaining a shed. The first stick is installed under and over alternate threads, starting with the first thread. When turned up on its edge the first space or shed is made. Insert the shuttle below the shed stick and pull through to the opposite side. Push the stick upwards to the other end of the frame. Then insert the second stick, starting with the stick under the second thread. Bring it down firmly to push the weave into place, then turn it up on its edge to lift the warp threads not raised in the first shed. Return the shuttle through the second shed to the opposite side. Remove the second stick and push the weft into place with the first stick. The first stick is once again turned on its edge and the shuttle returned to the opposite side.

It should be noted that the first stick remains in the warp during the weaving process; the second stick is inserted in alternate rows. These movements are continued until the required length of fabric is woven. To ensure that the sides of the fabric remain straight, do not pull the weft threads too tightly. It is also necessary to end the weaving at a distance of at least 1 to 2 in. (25 to 50 mm) from the nails. This prevents the fabric from unravelling and also allows for neatening the edge.

When weaving is finished, remove the shed. Then remove the fabric by cutting the warp threads close to the nails. Warp ends may be darned into the back of the work, or knotted together in groups of two or more close to the edge of the work. Loose ends are cut close to the knots or left hanging as a fringe.

Although this method produces a basic plain weave the results need not be repetitive. Different textures can be created with a variety of threads. Experiments with mixtures of matt and shiny threads, with knobbly and smooth threads and threads of different thickness, will produce a wide range of interesting effects. Other satisfying surface qualities can be achieved by weaving dried grasses, raffia, string, cord, strips of fabric, leather and plastic, ribbon and tape across a warp. The possible colour combinations of warp and weft threads is infinite. Warp and weft threads of equal thickness are both visible to the same extent. It should therefore be possible to create many subtle or bold changes of colour.

Woven fabrics resulting from these experiments can be used in embroidery as a background fabric for a design or used in any of the applied techniques.

TIE DYEING

In this method of decorating fabric patterns are produced by tying portions of the fabric with thread and string before immersing it in the dye. Threads and string are removed after dyeing, leaving parts of the fabric undyed. The undyed areas are ordered into patterns by varying the method and arrangement of the ties.

Tie dyeing lends itself well to use in embroidery. Patterned fabrics can be created for use as a background or for patchwork, appliqué and quilting. Semi-transparent and opaque fabrics, silk and cotton organdie, pure cotton fabrics, fine linen, shantung and 'Jap' (or lining) silk are particularly suitable for tie dyeing.

The materials and equipment necessary are simple. They consist of fabric, several weights of thread (twine, string, and cord) and hot-water dye ('Dylon' is boilable, permanent and easily obtained). It is important to know the nature of the fibres used in the construction of the fabric, as different dyes are required for natural and synthetic materials. Before the fabric is tied and dyed, it should be washed to remove starch or dressing – these act as a resist and prevent even dyeing. A stainless steel or similar metal bucket or bowl for boiling the fabric and dye is required. Some source of heat is essential; the hot plate or gas ring of a household cooker is suitable.

Tie dyeing is a 'free technique' and patterns cannot be planned too precisely. But the ties can be organized and planned so that patterns fall within certain areas of the fabric. Over-all striped patterns are created by rolling or pleating the fabric and tying bands of thread tightly in the areas which are to resist the dye. Different effects are achieved when the fabric is rolled or pleated either vertically, horizontally or diagonally to the shape of the piece of fabric. Circular patterns are created when the fabric is gathered up from the centre of the piece into a loose bunch and tied tightly with two or more bands of thread. Repeat patterns are produced by tying small bunches of the fabric wherever the repeat patterns are required. The bunches can be in ordered or random sequence. It is worth noting that the finer the thread or twine used, the more delicate and intricate is the effect. Bolder patterns are created by using thicker twine or cord and tying up larger areas of the fabric.

The method for tie dyeing is straightforward. When the fabric has been tied in the required manner, it is moistened and immersed in the dye bath. Mix the dye and use according to the manufacturer's instructions. When the dyeing is complete rinse the fabric in cold water to remove excess colour. Remove the ties and dry the fabric. Wash it in a mild solution of soap and warm water and press while damp.

Dyes are transparent and one colour dyed over another results in a

Tie dying lends itself well to use in embroidery and related techniques such as appliqué, patchwork and quilting. Although its effect cannot be precisely controlled, it is easy to do and produces a variety of striped and circular patterns. Here stripes of colour are alternated with lines of twisted chain stitch (page 96) and bordered by circular patterns of french knots and padding. Tie dye and embroidery 14 × 12 in. (355 × 305 mm).

third colour. It is necessary to protect (bind with threads) all areas of the fabric to remain the same colour. The procedure for dyeing several colours is illustrated here by the tying and dyeing procedure for three colours. First, tie the fabric to protect the areas which are to remain the initial colour of the fabric (white) and dye the first colour. Second, tie the fabric to protect the white areas and the areas to remain the first colour. Then dye the second colour. Third, tie the areas of fabric to remain white and the first and second colours, and dye the fabric the third colour. Between each stage of tying and dyeing, the fabric is rinsed, untied and dried as described above.

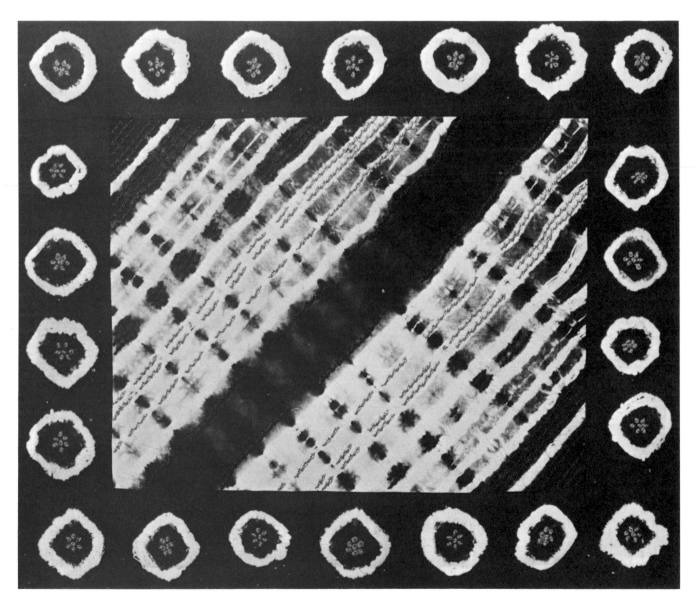

BATIK

Batik is an ancient method of decorating cloth that originated in Indonesia. It is based on the principle that grease and water do not mix. Designs and patterns are produced by applying wax to cloth and immersing the fabric in dye. The parts covered with wax do not receive the dye, but the wax becomes cracked during the dyeing process, and the dye seeps into the cracks producing the veining effect characteristic of batik.

For the embroiderer batik is an ideal method for producing patterned fabrics of original design, since it requires very little specialized equipment. The technique gives interesting effects on both semi-transparent and opaque fabrics, cotton sheeting, shantung and 'Jap' (lining) silk. It can be used to create patterned fabric for appliqué, patchwork and quilting, and for embroidery grounds. The characteristic veining can be used to advantage, being developed or enhanced by the addition of hand and machine stitchery.

Some form of heating equipment is required. The hot plate or gas ring of a household cooker can be used. Since the wax must be kept hot during the working process it is essential to site a flat working surface near to the source of heat. Melt the wax (household candles or paraffin wax) in a can placed in a saucepan partially filled with water. Mix the dye in a plastic bucket or bowl, according to the manufacturer's instructions. (Cold-water dyes must be used for batik; dyes that require boiling will melt the wax. 'Dylon' cold-water dyes are permanent and easily obtained). Wash the fabric to remove dressing and starch since dressing acts as a resist and prevents even dyeing. When the fabric is dry lay it flat on a working surface or stretch and pin it (with drawing pins, thumb tacks) to a wooden frame. With a bristle brush or tjanting apply the melted wax to those parts of the fabric which are not required to receive the dye. Either artists' or decorators' brushes are suitable and a variety of sizes could be useful. The tjanting is a traditional tool designed especially for use with melted wax. It consists of a handle on which is mounted a metal reservoir with a spout. It is easier to achieve fine lines using a tjanting. Place the waxed fabric in the dye and leave for thirty minutes, turning occasionally to ensure an even dye. Remove the fabric and dry.

If the fabric is to be dyed with a second colour, cover the areas to remain the first colour with wax and repeat the dyeing process. When producing a design of several colours the fabric should be absolutely dry before each new layer of wax is applied. If it is wet the wax will not penetrate the fabric, the dye will seep under it and the desired effect will be lost.

When all colours have been dyed the wax can be removed in one of

137

to thin it down with a little water to the right consistency for painting on fabric. Paint the design on the fabric. Fix water-based fabric dyes by ironing the reverse side of the work at the temperature appropriate for the particular fabric.

PASTEL DYES

These are particularly successful for creating spontaneous and free designs and there are several commercially manufactured types on the market. Some work on synthetic fabrics only and others on natural fibres. 'Pentel Dyeing Pastels' are easy to use. The design is drawn directly on to the fabric and made permanent with a hot iron. Iron over the right side of the work first and then over the reverse side. These pastels are intended for use on fabrics consisting of natural fibres, but they can be used on those consisting of a mixture of synthetic and natural fibres if the fabric responds well to a hot iron. Fabrics made entirely of synthetic fibres will not respond successfully to a hot iron.

Other pastel dyes are based on the transfer method. The design is drawn on to paper and the paper is then placed with the design face downwards on the fabric. The design is transferred to the fabric by ironing over the back of the paper. When the paper is removed the design is in reverse on the fabric. If a 'positive' is required, make two tracings, as described on page 34.

THE USE OF MACRAMÉ, KNITTING AND CROCHET WITH EMBROIDERY

These techniques further extend the range of textured and patterned fabrics available to the embroiderer.

Macramé

When designing a combination of macramé and embroidered fabric, perhaps for a decorative wall hanging, it is worth considering some of the possible ways of achieving a successful result before embarking on the actual work. One way would be to suspend a macramé structure consisting, for example, of open spaces and closely knotted areas against a fabric created with embroidery techniques. An alternative would be to design a hanging divided into alternating strips of embroidery and macramé. Another method would be to mount pieces of macramé on to an embroidery background, allowing them to hang loosely on the surface.

Whichever approach is chosen both techniques should work together

A decorative wall hanging, 9 × 17¼ in. (230 × 438 mm), on which macramé has been combined with stitchery and appliqué on a background of cotton curtain fabric. The stitches continue and develop the pattern of the macramé fringe.

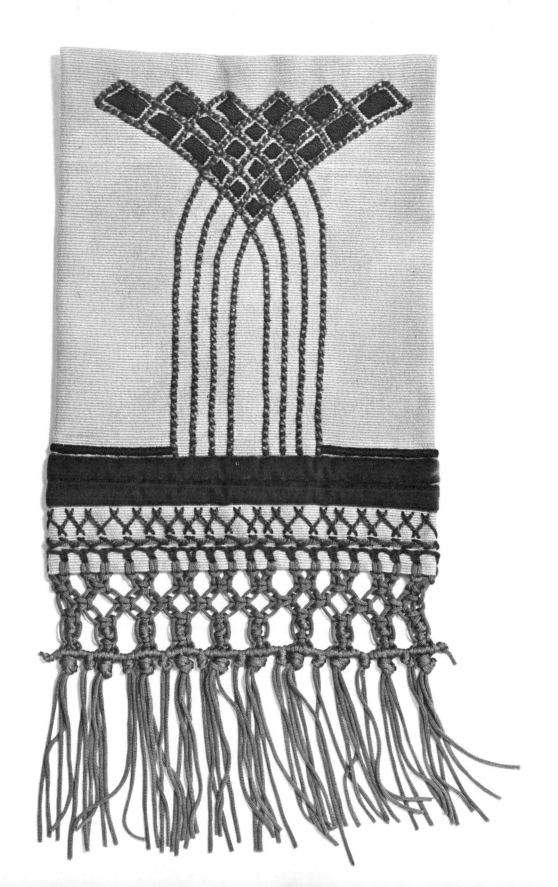

to create a cohesive whole. The knotted and ribbed effects of macramé can be echoed in embroidery with knotted stitches, cord, quilting, couched threads and cords. Pattern in macramé can be reflected in the embroidery by creating similar patterns with stitches and couched threads. Macramé using fine strands of cord and thread can be complemented with similar thickness of thread in the embroidery. Thin threads tend to lose their significance when placed in close proximity to over-large threads, although with experiment a reasonable balance between different sizes of threads can be achieved.

Knitting and appliqué by Carol Chorley, 8 × 5 in. (203 × 130 mm). Hand-knitted fabric is used as a background for applied shapes of cotton. The pattern of the knitting has been picked up by lines of running stitches in wool thread. It is advisable to knit pieces for appliqué and patchwork to the required size and shape so that they do not have to be cut in order to fit the design.

Knitting

The structure of a knitted fabric is not as close and firm as plain woven fabrics. The loop formation of knitting creates a non-stable structure which can be distorted by tension to a greater degree than a tightly

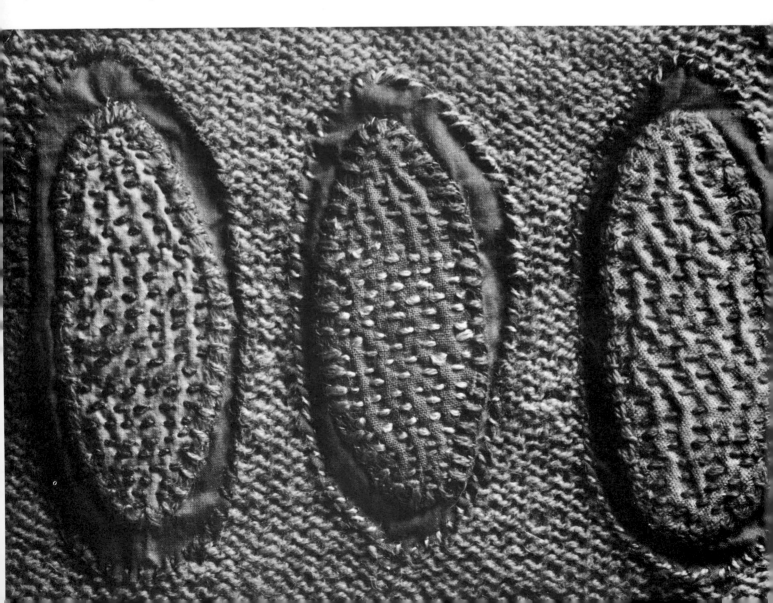

Fan by Gloria Marsh, 15 × 9 in. (380 × 230 mm). This fascinating embroidery consists of small fans applied to a background of cotton/wool fabric stitched over card. Each fan has been decorated with machine embroidery (presser-foot-in-position method) and a miniature hand-knitted glove. The shiny knitting thread used gives the design a contrast of texture and surface quality.

interlaced woven fabric. The degree of non-stability or stretch is determined by the nature and thickness of thread and the size of needle. The texture of a knitted fabric is the direct result of the structure. Threads are looped and twisted in various ways to create different effects. Pattern is achieved through the arrangement of different sequences of loops and twists together with colour.

Knitted fabrics can be used for many of the techniques of embroidery, in ways similar to woven fabrics. Most hand-knitted fabrics do not respond well to being cut, and of course threads cannot be withdrawn without destroying the structure of the fabric. When using hand-knitted fabrics in patchwork and appliqué, it is advisable to knit them to the required size and shape demanded by the design, always bearing in mind the different effects obtained with different sized needles. Hand-knitted fabrics are best used in crazy patchwork, or mosaic patchwork consisting of simple geometric shapes. It is difficult to knit more complex geometric shapes with success. Patches can be made to the correct size and overcast together on the wrong side of the work.

The instability of a very loosely knitted fabric can be manipulated to achieve very interesting effects. Such fabrics can be deliberately distorted when held in tension on frames or sewn to firm, stable fabric. Striped patterns can be pulled out of line to create curving bands. If such fabrics are supported below with a woven material, design and pattern can be developed and enriched with hand stitches and by applying beads, cords, ribbon and threads to the surface. Twine, raffia, strips of leather and fabric, cords and ribbon could be woven into knitted fabric.

Crochet

Crochet is easy to work and a quick method for producing interesting fabrics, small and large motifs and three-dimensional structures.

Open net-like and lacy crochet structures (either flat surfaces or three-dimensional forms) can be combined with commercially manufactured net and lace fabrics to achieve elaborate and detailed pattern effects. The results of such combinations can be developed further and enriched with the addition of stitchery.

Effects of depth are created when several layers of net and lace fabrics (crochet) are placed one over the other: the effect can be emphasized by separating the layers. This is done by stretching each layer over a separate frame. The frames are then placed one over the other and screwed together to form one unit. These designs may require the addition of other techniques, apart from stitchery. The back of the whole unit can be covered with fabric worked in any of the techniques of embroidery. Areas of each frame could be partially covered with fabric also worked with various kinds of embroidery. Cutwork, drawn thread and pulled work will combine satisfactorily with net and open patterns of crochet.

Detached motifs worked in crochet (lacy or close and firm) can be applied to a flat surface or the surface of three-dimensional forms to give interesting raised effects. There are several ways in which they can be attached. A few stitches worked in the centre of each motif will leave the edges free to stand away from the surface, adding a play of light and shade to the work. Motifs could be padded and applied in the ways described on pages 66 to 69.

Close, firm fabrics created in crochet, using a variety of threads, provide a rich source of interesting textures. Such fabrics can be used successfully in appliqué, patchwork and padding techniques. Like knitted fabrics, pieces of crochet intended for appliqué and patchwork can be made to the size required for a particular design, i.e., without a turning allowance. Patches of crochet can be joined edge to edge with overcast stitch.

Bibliography

Butler, Anne *Simple Stitches* London: Batsford 1968; *Embroidery Stitches: An Illustrated Guide* New York: Praeger 1968

Colby, Averil *Patchwork* London: Batsford 1958; Newton Centre, Mass.: Branford 1958

Colby, Averil *Quilting* London: Batsford 1972; New York: Scribner 1971

Green, David *Fabric Printing and Dyeing: A Practical Handbook* London: MacGibbon & Kee 1972; Newton Centre, Mass.: Branford 1972

Howard, Constance *Inspiration for Embroidery* London: Batsford 1967; Newton Centre, Mass.: Branford 1967

Kafka, Francis J. *Hand Decoration of Fabrics* London: Dover Publications 1974; New York: Dover Publications 1973

Krevitsky, Nik *Stitchery* London: Van Nostrand Reinhold 1966; *Stitchery: Art and Craft* New York: Van Nostrand Reinhold 1973

Laury, Jean Ray *Quilts and Coverlets: A Contemporary Approach* London: Van Nostrand Reinhold 1971; New York: Van Nostrand Reinhold 1970

Maile, Anne *Tie-and-dye as a Present Day Craft* London: Mills and Boon 1967; New York: Taplinger 1963 (Paperback: Ballantine 1971)

Marein, Shirley *Off the Loom: Creating with Fibre* London: Studio Vista 1972; New York: The Viking Press 1972

Meilach, Dona Z. *Contemporary Batik and Tie-Dye* London: Allen & Unwin 1973; New York: Crown 1972

Risley, Christine *Creative Embroidery* London: Studio Vista 1969; *Technique of Creative Embroidery* New York: Watson-Guptill 1969

Safford, Carleton and Bishop, Robert *America's Quilts and Coverlets* New York: Dutton 1972

Sausmarez, Maurice de *Basic Design: The Dynamics of Visual Form* London: Studio Vista 1964; New York: Van Nostrand Reinhold 1964

Short, Eirian *Introducing Macramé* London: Batsford 1970; New York: Watson-Guptill 1970 (Paperback: Fawcett World 1971)

Slade, Richard *Geometrical Patterns* London: Faber 1970; Levittown, N.Y.: Transatlantic 1970

Springall, Diana *Canvas Embroidery* London: Batsford 1969; Newton Centre, Mass.: Branford 1969

Thomas, Mary *Dictionary of Embroidery Stitches* London: Hodder and

Stoughton 1934; New York: Morrow 1935

Thomas, Richard K. *Three-Dimensional Design: A Cellular Approach* London: Van Nostrand Reinhold 1969; New York: Van Nostrand Reinhold 1969

Timmins, Alice *Introducing Patchwork* London: Batsford 1972; New York: Watson-Guptill 1968

Suppliers

GREAT BRITAIN

Embroidery threads, tools and equipment
C & F HANDICRAFT SUPPLIERS LTD, 346 Stag Lane, Kingsbury, London NW9 9AG (bulk suppliers)
DRYAD LTD, Cumberland Street, Northgates, Leicester, Leicestershire LE1 4QR
LOUISE GROSSÉ LTD, 36 Manchester Street, London W1M 5PE
MACCULLOUCH AND WALLIS LTD, 25/26 Dering Street, London W1E 0BH (machine embroidery cotton and metallic threads)
MACE AND NAIRN, 89 Crane Street, Salisbury, Wiltshire SP1 2PY
THE NEEDLEWOMAN SHOP, 146/148 Regent Street, London W1R 6BA

Fabrics
JOHN LEWIS & CO. LTD, Oxford Street, London W1A 1EX (calico, interlining, lining, dress and furnishing fabrics)
LOUISE GROSSÉ LTD, 36 Manchester Street, London W1M 5PE
MACCULLOUCH AND WALLIS LTD, 25/26 Dering Street, London W1E 0BH (interlinings, linings and calico)

Beads, sequins, paste
ELLS AND FARRIER LTD, 5 Princes Street, Hanover Square, London W1R 8PH

Wadding, kapok
JOHN LEWIS & CO. LTD, Oxford Street, London W1A 1EX
MACCULLOUCH AND WALLIS LTD, 25/26 Dering Street, London W1E 0BH

Quilting wool
THE NEEDLEWOMAN SHOP, 146/148 Regent Street, London W1R 6BA

Leather, skins
LIGHT LEATHER CO. LTD, 18 Newman Street, London W1P 3HD
LOUISE GROSSÉ LTD, 36 Manchester Street, London W1M 5PE (gold and silver kid)

Weaving yarn, rug wool
CRAFTSMAN'S MARK YARNS LTD, Bronberllen, Trefnant, Denbighshire, North Wales

DRYAD LTD, Cumberland Street, Northgates, Leicester, Leicestershire LE1 4QR

THE NEEDLEWOMAN SHOP, 146/148 Regent Street, London W1R 6BA (rug wool, knitting wool)

THE WEAVERS SHOP, King Street, Wilton, Salisbury, Wiltshire SP2 0AY

Dye, wax, batik equipment

CANDLE MAKERS SUPPLIES, 4 Beaconsfield Terrace Road, London W14 0PP

DRYAD LTD, Cumberland Street, Northgates, Leicester, Leicestershire LE1 4QR

DYLON INTERNATIONAL LTD, Worsley Bridge Road, London SE26 5HD

UNITED STATES

Embroidery threads, tools and equipment

HERRSCHNERS NEEDLECRAFTS, Hoover Road, Stevens Point, WI 54481

LEE WARDS, CREATIVE CRAFTS CENTER, 12 St Charles Street, Elgin, IL 60120 (mail order)

MERRIBEE NEEDLECRAFT COMPANY, 2904 West Lancaster, Fort Worth, TX 76107 (mail order)

Weaving yarn

FIBRE YARN CO. INC., 840 Sixth Avenue, New York, NY 10009

LILY MILLS COMPANY, Handweaving Department, Shelby, NC 28150 (yarns, macramé cords, small looms: mail order)

PATERNAYAN BROS. INC., 312 East 95th Street, New York, NY 10028 (rug, tapestry and crewel wool)

THE YARN DEPOT INC., 545 Sutter Street, San Francisco, CA 94102

Dye, wax, batik tools

CRAFTWORK INC., 1 Industrial Avenue, Woodbridge, New Jersey

ARTHUR BROWN AND BRO. INC., 2 West 46th Street, New York, NY 10036

Index